D1153913

Social Issues
in Literature

Bioethics in Mary Shelley's *Frankenstein*

Other Books in the Social Issues in Literature Series:

Social Issues
in Literature

Bioethics in Mary
Shelley's *Frankenstein*

Gary Wiener, Book Editor

GREENHAVEN PRESS
A part of Gale, Cengage Learning

GALE
CENGAGE Learning™

Detroit • New York • San Francisco • New Haven, Conn • Waterville, Maine • London

Christine Nasso, *Publisher*
Elizabeth Des Chenes, *Managing Editor*

© 2011 Greenhaven Press, a part of Gale, Cengage Learning

Gale and Greenhaven Press are registered trademarks used herein under license.

For more information, contact:
Greenhaven Press
27500 Drake Rd.
Farmington Hills, MI 48331-3535
Or you can visit our Internet site at gale.cengage.com

Articles in Greenhaven Press anthologies are often edited for length to meet page require-ments. In addition, original titles of these works are changed to clearly present the main thesis and to explicitly indicate the author's opinion. Every effort is made to ensure that Greenhaven Press accurately reflects the original intent of the authors. Every effort has been made to trace the owners of copyrighted material.

Cover image © Photos 12/Alamy.

LIBRARY OF CONGRESS CATALOGING-IN-PUBLICATION DATA

Bioethics in Mary Shelley's Frankenstein / Gary Wiener, book editor.
    p. cm. -- (Social issues in literature)
  Includes bibliographical references and index.
  ISBN 978-0-7377-5012-6 (hardcover) -- ISBN 978-0-7377-5013-3 (pbk.)
  1. Shelley, Mary Wollstonecraft, 1797-1851. Frankenstein. 2. Shelley, Mary Woll-stonecraft, 1797-1851--Knowledge--Science. 3. Science fiction, English--History and criticism. 4. Bioethics in literature. 5. Scientists in literature. 6. Science in lit-erature. 7. Monsters in literature. 8. Frankenstein, Victor (Fictitious character) 9. Frankenstein's monster (Fictitious character) I. Wiener, Gary. II. Series: Social is-sues in literature.
  PR5397.F733B56 2010
  823'.7--dc22
                                                                    2010020229

Printed in the United States of America
2 3 4 5 6 7 14 13 12 11 10

Contents

The inspiration for Mary Shelley's creation of protagonist Victor Frankenstein may have been Dr. James Lind—a mentor to Percy Bysshe Shelley—whose interest in animal electricity led him to perform galvanic experiments.

Mary Shelley was not warning of unchecked scientific pursuit as much as she was of Romantic egotism. The evolution of film creatures from demons to protagonists has helped to refocus the popular conception of the novel.

Chapter 3: Contemporary Perspectives on Bioethics

Introduction

Mary Shelley's unnamed creature, which she conceived in response to poet Lord Byron's challenge to write a ghost story in the summer of 1816, has taken on a life of its own. Inevitably the book that Shelley referred to as her "hideous progeny" will be better known and more widely circulated in the year 2018 than it was in 1818, when it was first published. How is it that this monster story continues to make itself relevant for each new era? The answer lies in Shelley's uncanny ability to portend a future in which artificial bipeds will walk the earth, in which scientists will create artificial limbs and organs, in which doctors will transplant new organs to replace those that have failed, in which xenotransplantation (or the use of animal parts—such as a baboon's heart—in human beings) will increase steadily, and in which animals and perhaps even humans will be cloned. As University of Wisconsin Professor of Medical History and Bioethics Susan Lederer writes, "Over the course of the twentieth century, the atomic bomb, organ transplants, xenografting . . . genetic engineering, in vitro fertilization, and most recently, cloning have all provoked comparisons to the Frankenstein myth." The repercussions of such biotechnological advances pose myriad ethical challenges, and thus we have the continued relevance of what many have called the first science fiction novel.

Originally published anonymously in part because the creation of such a tale by a young woman was considered somewhat monstrous in itself, *Frankenstein* is the story of the eponymous doctor, Victor Frankenstein, who sets out to solve what so many before and after him have wrestled with: the mystery of mortality and how to ensure eternal life. In Victor's words, "I entered with the greatest diligence into the search of the philosopher's stone and the elixir of life; but the latter soon obtained my undivided attention. Wealth was an inferior object, but what glory would attend the discovery if I could banish disease from the human frame and render man invulnerable to any but a violent death!" Victor soon realizes that his work is more gory than glorious:

> Who shall conceive the horrors of my secret toil as I dabbled among the unhallowed damps of the grave or tortured the living animal to animate the lifeless clay? My limbs now tremble, and my eyes swim with the remembrance; but then a resistless, and almost frantic, impulse, urged me forward; I seemed to have lost all soul or sensation but for this one pursuit. It was indeed but a passing trance, that only made me feel with renewed acuteness so soon as, the unnatural stimulus ceasing to operate, I had returned to my old habits. I collected bones from charnel-houses and disturbed, with profane fingers, the tremendous secrets of the human frame. In a solitary chamber, or rather cell, at the top of the house, and separated from all the other apartments by a gallery and staircase, I kept my workshop of filthy creation; my eye-balls were starting from their sockets in attending to the details of my employment. The dissecting room and the slaughter-house furnished many of my materials; and often did my human nature turn with loathing from my occupation, whilst, still urged on by an eagerness which perpetually increased, I brought my work near to a conclusion.

But Victor is appalled at his own creation from the first moments he sees it come alive and walk. He runs in panic from his offspring, as well as from his responsibility toward this newly minted monster, and thus begins a story that leads to inevitable tragedy.

So began as well the mad scientist mythology forever after associated with Mary Shelley's protagonist. As Leslie Fiedler writes:

> [Shelley] never refers to Frankenstein as a "doctor"—calling him only "Victor" or "Baron." But in the popular mind he rapidly came to be thought of as, and has remained forever,

"Dr." Frankenstein. . . . It seems a little surprising all the same that *Frankenstein* so deeply moved its readers long before the Hospital had become a major institution, the practice of medicine a prestigious and rewarding . . . profession, health care a large part of every national budget, and bioethics a subject of obsessive concern.

As Fiedler notes, however, Shelley's novel has never gone out of print in the almost two hundred years since its publication and, moreover, has become an essentially mythic work, existing out of time, "in the eternal now of the collective unconscious."

So it should be no surprise that "the shadow of Frankenstein looms over us far into the horizon," as Walter James Miller writes in his foreword to the Signet edition of the novel. "Continually," Miller asserts, "it haunts us in the news." With every breakthrough in cloning, Miller says, we are warned of "Frankenstein-type people." With every genetically modified edible, demonstrators warn of "Frankenfoods." And with every dubious or uncertain advance in science, newspapers sport headlines such as this 2000 article from *The New York Times*: "Dr. Frankenstein, Please Call Your Office."

Despite the cavalier manner with which the guardians of bioethics toss around dire warnings and vilify legitimate scientists, one may argue whether Shelley's novel is a valid text by which to assess contemporary science. After all, Victor Frankenstein commits a number of mistakes besides simply creating artificial life: he works alone without checks, balances, or supervision; he abdicates responsibility for the creature once it stands up and walks; he decides not to notify the authorities of what he has perpetrated even when he has the chance; and he adopts an arrogant and egotistical attitude, obstinately refusing to consider his situation from all perspectives. For example, when the monster informs Victor that "I will be with you on your wedding-night," the scientist egocentrically decides that the monster will kill him at that time. To his dismay Victor realizes too late that the monster's intended victim is his bride, Elizabeth. Science writer Stephen Jay Gould even challenges the basic premise behind the Frankenstein bioethical argument, declaring that the monster turned evil not due to a failed experiment but because his creator rejected him based on his appearance.

Given all of these factors and, moreover, because *Frankenstein* is, after all, merely speculative fiction, Susan Tyler Hitchcock, author of *Frankenstein: A Cultural History*, quotes an unnamed science writer who states unequivocally that no scientists working today "would take seriously a reference to *Frankenstein*" as a reason not to proceed with reasonable experimentation. The science writer goes on to state that "people with a political motive can play on the public's ignorance and whip up irrational fear by summoning up a popular myth or suggesting analogies to historic disasters and thereby engender reactions that are completely out of proportion to the risks."

Others are not so quick to dismiss the validity of the novel as a bioethical lesson for modern scientific practice. As James A. Metcalf, professor in the College of Health and Human Services at George Mason University, argues, "Mary Shelley was 200 years behind us technologically, but 200 years ahead of us philosophically." Though Metcalf acknowledges that Shelley's vision of "a crude collage of human scraps that were magically brought to life" is "ludicrously far-fetched in the twenty-first century mind," he believes that Shelley "engaged the same moral and ethical dilemmas that we must now contemplate within a scientific capability that far exceeds hers. What she contemplated in fantasy, we may have to contemplate in reality." As Metcalf concludes, "What is too often dismissed as irrelevant is eminently relevant, particularly to students of today's health care professions."

Dr. Cecil Helman, in his book *The Body of Frankenstein's Monster*, agrees. Bemoaning the state of a modern science that is creating bionic people, Hellman predicts that "one day puzzled archaeologists will sift, frowning, through the dusty gravesites of our culture. On the glass shelves of their great museums there will be no arrow heads or pottery or jade jewelry, but rather steel hip joints, plastic arteries, ceramic teeth, a metal heart, and a row of hearing aids." This world of artificial body parts is becoming the new reality, Helman asserts, making *Frankenstein* more relevant than ever.

Whether as the simple "ghost story" it was originally intended to be or as a dire prediction of science run amok, Mary Shelley's *Frankenstein* has never been easily dismissed. The original vision of a nineteen-year-old girl has garnered surprising popularity. By 1823, five years after its initial publication, a stage version was already playing in London, and many more were to follow. In the twentieth century, *Frankenstein* films and offshoots, that vary in style and substance from the original James Whale *Frankenstein* of 1931 to the campy *Rocky Horror Picture Show* of 1975, number in the dozens. The essays that follow suggest that *Frankenstein* is still a remarkably relevant text for our era. These viewpoints reflect our society's continuing interest in the scientific dilemma that Mary Shelley's novel posed almost two hundred years ago.

Chronology

1797
Mary Wollstonecraft Godwin is born August 30 in London, England. Her mother, Mary Wollstonecraft, dies on September 10.

1801
Mary's father, William Godwin, marries Mary Jane Clairmont.

1807
The Godwin family moves to Skinner Street, Holborn, London.

1808
Mary's poem "Mounseer Nongtongpaw" is published.

1812
Mary spends time in Scotland. Mary returns to London and meets the poet Percy Bysshe Shelley.

1814
Mary elopes with Percy Shelley.

1815
Mary gives birth to their first child, who dies shortly after.

1816
Mary gives birth to William Shelley. Mary begins *Frankenstein*. Percy's first wife, Harriet, commits suicide; her body is found on December 10. Mary and Percy marry on December 30.

1817
History of a Six Weeks' Tour is published. Mary finishes *Frankenstein*. Mary gives birth to Clara Shelley.

1818

The first edition of *Frankenstein* is published. Clara Shelley dies.

1819

Mary completes her novella *Mathilda*. William Shelley dies. Mary gives birth to Percy Florence. He is her only child to survive to adulthood.

1822

Percy Bysshe Shelley drowns in Italy.

1823

Valperga is published.

1826

The Last Man is published.

1835

Lodore is published.

1836

William Godwin dies.

1837

Falkner is published.

1839

Mary publishes Percy Shelley's *Poetical Works*.

1840–1843

Mary travels throughout Europe.

1844

Rambles in Germany and Italy is published.

1851
Mary dies at age fifty-three.

1959
Mathilda is published.

Background on
Mary Shelley

The Life of Mary Shelley

Authors and Artists for Young Adults

According to this viewpoint, even if Mary Shelley had never written a novel, she would have achieved notoriety for other reasons. She was the daughter of two famous parents—the philosopher and writer William Godwin and his wife, the influential feminist and author of A Vindication of the Rights of Woman, *Mary Wollstonecraft—and she married the English Romantic poet Percy Bysshe Shelley. There is, to her credit, one further reason for Mary's enduring fame: the monster she dreamed up when she was eighteen years old, during the summer of 1816, which she spent on Lake Geneva in Switzerland. Despite the incredible success of* Frankenstein *and its entry into literary and popular culture, Shelley remains a minor figure in the English literary pantheon because none of her subsequent works ever met with the success of her first novel.*

Mary Shelly's personal life rivals anything she ever wrote. Her parents were Mary Wollstonecraft and William Godwin, both intellectual rebels of the closing of the eighteenth century. Wollstonecraft was the author of *A Vindication of the Rights of Woman*, an early feminist tract with much influence in its day and still "required reading for studies in women's rights," according to [biographer Muriel] Spark. Godwin was both a political philosopher and novelist, author of *Enquiry Concerning Political Justice* and the novel *Caleb Williams*, among others. These two did not simply write about a new society; they lived it. Wollstonecraft, spirited though often depressed, had a child, Fanny, out of wedlock during her years in Paris reporting on the French revolution. When Godwin met her in the summer of 1796, there was an immediate attraction. The couple at first set up separate houses near each other, then with the coming of a child, Godwin relented in his opposition to marriage, and they wed in March of 1797, just five months before the birth of Mary.

Mary's Early Life

Her birth, however, was a mixed blessing for Godwin, for his wife died eleven days later from puerperal fever [a sometimes fatal genital tract infection affecting women shortly after childbirth], and Godwin was left to care for the baby and her three-year-old half-sister. For the next several years he supervised all aspects of her care, and the two became inseparable. This tight bond was severed, however, when Godwin remarried to Mary Jane Clairmont in 1801. This stepmother brought a six-year-old son and four-year-old daughter into the union, and according to most accounts she had none of the finer sensibilities of Mary's biological mother. The new Mrs. Godwin was, according to such accounts, something of a dragon regarding Mary—making her do the housework while sending her own daughter Jane to boarding school. Mary was, in fact, educated at home but was fortunate to have her father's extensive library from which to choose volumes on topics from science to philosophy. There were also visitors to the house who provided intellectual stimulation—men such as William Wordsworth and Samuel Taylor Coleridge. She heard Coleridge recite his *Rime of the Ancient Mariner* while hiding in the parlor with her stepsister, Jane, an early influence that would affect her later writing, most especially sections of *Frankenstein*. Other biographers have also noted that Mary inherited a pessimistic, depressed side to her character from her mother, spending many hours at her mother's grave reading from Wollstonecraft's works.

Godwin meanwhile, upon the insistence of his new wife, had begun a commercial enterprise in publishing with his Juvenile Library. One of Mary's favorite pastimes as a child was

Mary Wollstonecraft Shelley. © Bettmann/Corbis.

writing stories, and a reworking of a popular song into a long poem, *Mounseer Nongtongpaw*, became her first published work under her father's imprint. She was eleven at the time, and the work was popular enough to be republished in 1830 with illustrations by Robert Cruikshank, who illustrated much of [novelist Charles] Dickens's work. "It is not singular, that, as the daughter of two persons of distinguished literary celebrity, I should early in life have thought of writing," Shelley noted in her 1831 introduction to *Frankenstein*. In 1812, Godwin, influenced by his wife, sent Mary to friends in Scotland, where she remained until the summer of 1814, with only occasional visits to her home in London. These years helped nurture her literary imagination as well as give her a sense of freedom, away from her stepmother.

Percy Bysshe Shelley Complicates Mary's Relationships

Mary first met the poet Percy Bysshe Shelley in London on an 1812 visit home. Shelley, the son of a wealthy aristocrat, was a new disciple to Godwin's free-thinking creed, though it was not until Mary's final return home in 1814 that the two became attracted to each other. Shelley was married, the father of one child and another on the way, but he had grown weary of his wife and believed, as Godwin also espoused, in a higher morality than society's. The young poet visited Godwin's regularly, and Mary—chaperoned by her stepsister Jane—walked with him and paid visits to her mother's grave at St. Pancras Church. By the end of June they had declared their love for each other and when Godwin found out, he banned Shelley from the house. Young Mary was torn between love for her father and for Shelley, but soon followed her heart. An attempted suicide by the poet convinced her of his love and, accompanied by Jane, the couple fled to France on July 28, 1814. Mary was only sixteen at the time.

The next nine years, except for two interludes in England, were spent traveling in Europe, throughout Switzerland, Germany, and Italy. They were also characterized by poverty and domestic tragedy, by both romance and high melodrama. Living partnered without the benefit of marriage, Percy Shelley was cut off by his outraged father from any but a meager allowance, yet he and Mary, accompanied by Jane (who ultimately renamed herself Claire) travelled extensively in the summer of 1814 before returning to England in the fall, enough to give Mary Shelley material for a travel book, *History of a Six Weeks' Tour*, ultimately published in 1817 and written largely from journals of the time and from letters sent home to her half-sister, Fanny.

Yet this was in the future: for the present Mary Shelley was pregnant, living in poverty in England with her common-law husband, often in hiding to avoid arrest for nonpayment of debts. In quieter times the couple continued their ambitious course of study in the classics and contemporary literature. Encouraged by her husband, Shelley also started a historical novel left unfinished as her pregnancy ended in a premature birth of a daughter in February, 1815. The baby died twelve days later. In her journal of March 19, 1815, Shelley recorded the following dream, a possible inspiration for *Frankenstein*: "Dream that my little baby came to life again—that it had only been cold & that we rubbed it before the fire & it lived." The reality was that the couple tried to pick up their old life again. "Read and talk," Shelley wrote in her journal. "Still think about my little baby—'tis hard, indeed, for a mother to lose a child." She would have more practice at such loss in the coming years. Complicating Shelley's life was the continual presence of her stepsister who had a decided affection for Percy Shelley, one that he, imbued with a passion for free love, did little to discourage. In fact, he urged Mary Shelley into an affair with his friend, [British writer Thomas] Jefferson Hogg, not long after the death of their first child.

Inspiration for *Frankenstein*

A second child, William, was born in January of 1816 and in the following May the family departed for Geneva where they were to meet up with George Gordon, Lord Byron, stepsister Claire's new love interest and one of the most celebrated literary figures in all of Europe. And it was there that Mary Shelley began composition of her novel.... Initially the story of Victor Frankenstein and his creation seemed to her to be but a short tale, but encouraged by her husband, she developed the story at greater length....

Shelley worked on the novel partially during the time of her third pregnancy. The book was finished in May of 1817, and her daughter, Clara Everina, was born in September of that year. During this same time she also put together the travel book, *History of a Six Weeks' Tour*, published in late 1817. The couple had returned to England the year before, where more sadness awaited them. In October of 1816, Mary's half-sister Fanny killed herself, a terrible echo of her mother's two attempts at suicide, and Percy Shelley's wife died. This last event left the couple free to wed, which they did on December 30, 1816. The legitimacy of marriage improved their financial position somewhat with Percy Shelley's father.

Publication of *Frankenstein* occurred on New Year's Day of 1818. Its author's identity was at first unknown, though many assumed it to be by Percy Shelley. Critical response was mixed at the time, from those who thought the author had created a sensationalist and gruesome tract, to those who felt the anonymous author had great powers of imagination and description. Later critics tended to concentrate more on the philosophical impact of the novel, focusing on the subtitle, *The Modern Prometheus*, and examining the text for clues of unbridled creativity wreaking its own destruction. Still others have shown similarities in the novel to earlier Gothic horror novels such as Ann Radcliffe's *The Mysteries of Udolpho*, to books by Shelley's father, Godwin, including *Caleb* [Williams] and *Saint Leon*, and allusions to John Milton's *Paradise Lost*, [Johann Wolfgang von] Goethe's *Faust*, and Coleridge's *Rime of the Ancient Mariner*....

To Europe Once Again

In 1818 the Shelleys returned to Europe, settling in Italy for Percy Shelley's health, yet the move proved disastrous. Clara Everina, just a year old, died in Venice in September, and the son, William, died the following year in Rome. "You see by our hap how blind we mortals are when we go seeking after what we think our good," Shelley wrote in a letter. "But the Climate is not [by] any means warm enough to be of benefit to him & yet it is that that has destroyed my two children—We went from England comparatively prosperous and happy—I should return broken-hearted and miserable—. . . . I can assure you I am much changed—the world will ever be to me again as it was—" At twenty-two, Mary Shelley had already experienced enough tragedy for one lifetime. In ways she blamed the deaths of her children on her husband and from that time on she withdrew from him.

She also kept writing. A novella, *Mathilda*, was written during the late summer and fall of 1819, but never published in Shelley's lifetime. Basically the story of a father and daughter's incestuous attraction for each other, *Mathilda* is told in the form of memoirs addressed to a poet named Woodville—a stand-in for Percy Shelley—and written by a young woman who expects to die at age twenty-two. Largely autobiographical, the story traces the course of Mathilda's life, from her birth—which caused the death of her mother—through the abandonment by her beloved father when she is sent to Scotland, and through her return sixteen years later and the admission by her father of his incestuous love for her. Writing about the novel, published in 1959, [Anne K.] Mellor noted that *Mathilda* "calls into question the bourgeois sexual practices of her day." It was also full of anger and self-recrimination as Shelley was trying to come to terms with the deaths of her two children. The birth of her fourth and last child, Percy Florence, in November of 1819, in part helped to heal those emotional wounds.

By the spring of 1820, Shelley was hard at work on two blank-verse dramas from [ancient Roman poet] Ovid, *Proserpine* and *Midas*, as well as on another novel, *Valperga*. The latter was a historical novel about Castruccio, prince of Lucca, who returns to his native city after a life of exile and must choose between his love for Euthanasia and his search for absolute power.... Yet again, her writing was put on hold by tragedy. Settling in Pisa in 1821, the Shelleys were joined by Byron. Percy Shelley had formed liaisons with several other women, including stepsister Claire, since the time of his wife's cooling toward him. But with Byron's arrival at the end of the year, a spirit of literary camaraderie was once more established. This was cut short, however, with Mary Shelley's miscarriage in June, 1822, and then the death of her husband by drowning on July 8 while he was sailing in the Gulf of Spezia.

On Her Own

Mary Shelley was left now entirely on her own to raise her son. After a period of intense depression, she once again turned to writing not only for emotional succor but also for material sustenance. Her *Valperga* was published in 1823, the year she returned to England to live. The reception of her book was somewhat enhanced by a dramatic production of *Frankenstein* which had a prodigious success in London. None of Shelley's five other novels would be greeted with the critical success of her *Frankenstein*, however. Reviewers of the day could not help but compare *Valperga* to its author's first novel, as did a reviewer in *Blackwood's Edinburgh Magazine*: "*Valperga* is, for a second romance, by no means what its predecessor was for a first one." Most reviewers, then and now, agree that the novel is much too long....

In 1826 Shelley published *The Last Man*, something of an idealized picture of Percy Shelley in the guise of the last man left on earth after the destruction, by plague, of the human race in the twenty-first century. The book was also partly inspired by the death of Lord Byron in 1824. She wrote in her journal shortly after Byron's death: "The last man! Yes I may well describe that solitary being's feelings, feeling myself as the last relic of a beloved race, my companions extinct before me—" Recognized now as a prototype of the modern science fiction tale, *The Last Man* is Shelley's second-best known novel, and Shelley's "darkest and gloomiest," according to Eleanor Ty in *Dictionary of Literary Biography*....

In the 1820s, Shelley also turned her hand to journalism in an attempt to earn money, writing book reviews and cultural pieces for magazines such as *Examiner, London Magazine*, and *Westminster Review*. She also helped to edit the remaining manuscripts of Percy Shelley. However, the angry reaction of Sir Timothy Shelley to the appearance of his son's *Posthumous Poems* forced her to agree not to publish any more of her late husband's poems during the lifetime of Sir Timothy. In return, she won an annual allowance for her son.

A lesser known novel by Shelley is *The Fortunes of Perkin Warbeck* (1830), detailing the life of a man who claimed to have been the son of Edward IV, Duke of York, and thus a pretender to the throne. Shelley follows his fortunes from his escape from the Tower of London to his ultimate end on the scaffold. According to Ty in *Dictionary of Literary Biography*, *The Fortunes of Perkin Warbeck* was one of Shelley's "least successful" novels, inspired by [Scottish Romantic novelist] Sir Walter Scott's historical romances, but suffering from uninspired writing....

More overtly autobiographical novels are *Lodore* (1835) and *Falkner* (1837). These two repeat the triangle of mixed emotions between father, daughter, and lover that was initiated in *Mathilda*. With *Lodore*, Shelley created for the first time a happy ending, though one which Ty concluded was "sentimentalized and unrealistic." *Falkner* is a more clearly autobiographical piece, in which the Byronic protagonist, Falkner, is the guardian of orphaned Elizabeth and is also haunted by secrets in his past. When Elizabeth falls in love with the son of a woman Falkner once helped destroy, he is beset by guilt. Elizabeth is thus caught between her lover, who seeks revenge, and her adoptive father's obsession. According to Ty, *Falkner*, Shelley's last novel, is also one of her "best works."

Mary Shelley's Later Years

In 1831 came a revised edition of *Frankenstein* which helped Shelley's financial affairs, and beginning in 1834 she undertook a series of biographical sketches for the popular *Cabinet Cyclopedia* series, in addition to other journalistic chores. These mini-biographies increasingly became her bread and butter, and they included works on literary and scientific men of Italy, Spain, Portugal, and France. Indeed, Shelley's real skill as a journalist was in disseminating the cultural heritage of the continent to England. . . . Shelley's own description of these years can be found in her journals: "Routine occupation is the medicine of my mind. I write the 'Lives' in the morning. I read novels and memoirs of an evening—such is the variety of my days and time flies so swift, that days form weeks and weeks form months, before I am aware."

With her son at Harrow and then at Trinity College, Shelley was much occupied with a literary life. She never married again, and in later years dedicated her life to keeping her dead husband's name before the public. Sir Timothy eventually relented regarding publication of his son's poetry, and Mary Shelley became a tireless editor and literary historian, writing notes and prefaces to editions of his work that "provide the most thorough and reliable biographical background to [Percy] Shelley's poems of any single source," according to [John R.] Holmes. With the graduation of her son, Shelley's fortunes turned for the better—Sir Timothy endowed his grandson with a larger yearly stipend and he and his mother subsequently travelled together in Germany and Italy in the early 1840s, resulting in Shelley's final work, *Rambles in Germany and Italy*. By the time of its publication, however, Shelley was already suffering from poor health and beset by blackmailers who would plague her last years. After her son's marriage, Shelley lived with Percy Florence and his new wife. However, she soon began to exhibit symptoms of the brain tumor which eventually took her life on February 1, 1851.

Writing of Shelley's life, Leigh Hunt, poet and personal friend of Percy Shelley, once described the novelist as "four-famed." By this he meant her two famous parents, her poet husband, and the monster she had created. Alluding to this, Spark summed up Shelley's life, noting that she was not only the daughter of William Godwin and Mary Wollstonecraft, not only the wife of Shelley and mother of Sir Percy Shelley. "She was also a professional writer of lasting fame," Spark concluded, though, as [William A.] Walling has pointed out, a "minor figure" in English literature.

Mary Shelley Shared Victor Frankenstein's Interest in Science

Elizabeth Nitchie

Elizabeth Nitchie is the author of numerous books, including The Stage History of Frankenstein.

According to Nitchie in the following selection, it would have been impossible for young Mary Shelley to write so convincingly of Victor Frankenstein's scientific abilities had she not been interested in the scientific discoveries of her own day. Guided by her reading of British scientist Sir Humphry Davy and the experiments of Erasmus Darwin, as well as discussions between her husband, Percy Bysshe Shelley, and fellow poet Lord Byron, Shelley became fascinated with contemporary science. In particular, recent experiments in reanimating corpses via electrical charges spurred her creativity and led her to imagine Victor Frankenstein's creation of the monster. Shelley did not divulge the science that enabled Victor to discover the secret of life for obvious reasons, but her warning of the potential dangers of scientific discovery resounded in the works of later writers who were influenced by her novel. Shelley herself continued to revisit the subject of scientific discovery in later stories and in her novel The Last Man.

N o young woman could have written so effectively of [novel character Victor] Frankenstein's scientific curiosity unless she had shared it to some degree. Absorbing from her [Mary Shelley's] reading (she had read [British scientist Sir Humphry] Davy in October, 1816, while she was at work on

Elizabeth Nitchie, *Mary Shelley, Author of "Frankenstein."* Piscataway, NJ: Rutgers University Press, 1953. Copyright © 153 by Rutgers, the State University. Reproduced by permission of Rutgers University Press.

Frankenstein) and ... conversation ... some sense of what it meant to think at the same time scientifically and imaginatively, Mary set her lively mind to work on the possible results of research into the mystery of the life principle. It was the discussions at Lord [Byron's residence, Villa] Diodati about the origins of life and the experiments in galvanism that furnished the stimulus for the story of *Frankenstein*. The eager young people gathered in Byron's villa talked of [English physician] Erasmus Darwin and his reputed success in imparting life to a piece of vermicelli [pasta], of his "speculations on the resemblance between the action of the human soul and that of electricity." "Perhaps a corpse would be re-animated; galvanism had given token of such things: perhaps the component parts of a creature might be manufactured, brought together, and endued with vital warmth." Between sleeping and waking one night Mary had a vision of "the pale student of unhallowed arts kneeling beside the thing he had put together," and of his creature. Endowed with life, it frightened out of uneasy sleep both its creator and its creator's creator. She had found her "ghost story" to add to the abortive tales the others in the house party had already begun and abandoned. Mary's was to live in successive editions, in allusions, in stage plays, and even in moving pictures (which must "amuse" her in her grave) on through the first half of the twentieth century.

Victor as Scientist

Victor Frankenstein, the young Genevese student of natural philosophy, felt "the enticements of science," with its "continual food for discovery and wonder," comparing it with other studies in which the student goes only as far as others have gone before him. Always "embued with a fervent longing to penetrate the secrets of nature," he had his imagination first caught by the alchemists' search for the philosopher's stone and the elixir of life. He read avidly in the [physiological and occult] works of Cornelius Agrippa, Albertus Magnus, and

Lord Byron, Percy Bysshe Shelley, John Polidori, Mary Shelley, and Mary's stepsister Claire engaged in a written ghost story contest while staying at Villa Diodati (pictured) on Lake Geneva. The late-night conversations provided inspiration for Mary Shelley's novel Frankenstein. *© Interfoto/Alamy.*

Paracelsus. But modern science, as taught by Professor Waldman at [the University of] Ingolstadt, soon supplanted the ancient magic and put Victor's internal being into a state of turmoil. Waldman's opening lecture on chemistry concluded:

> The ancient teachers of this science promised impossibilities, and performed nothing. The modern masters promise very little; they know that metals cannot be transmuted, and that the elixir of life is a chimera. But these philosophers, whose hands seem only made to dabble in dirt, and their eyes to pore over the microscope or crucible, have indeed performed miracles. They penetrate into the recesses of nature, and show how she works in her hiding places. They ascend into the heavens: they have discovered how the blood circulates, and the nature of the air we breathe. They have acquired new and almost unlimited power; they can command the thunders of heaven, mimic the earthquake, and even mock the invisible world with its own shadows.

Guided and advised by Waldman to pursue every branch of natural philosophy, including mathematics, Frankenstein progressed rapidly until he became the equal of his professors. In his interest in the nature and origin of life, he began to study anatomy and physiology. "To examine the causes of life," he concluded, "we must first have recourse to death." In the graveyards and charnel houses he observed the corruption and decay of the human body. "I paused, examining and analyzing all the minutiae of causation, as exemplified in the change from life to death, and death to life, until from the midst of this darkness a sudden light broke in upon me. . . . After days and nights of incredible labour and fatigue, I succeeded in discovering the cause of generation and life; nay, more, I became myself capable of bestowing animation upon lifeless matter."

Creating a Monster

And so Frankenstein, gathering the parts from graves, created his Monster. Finally "on a dreary night in November," he "saw the dull yellow eye of the creature open; it breathed hard, and a convulsive motion agitated its limbs." What the life-giving process was, Mary does not allow Frankenstein to tell us, whether it was galvanism or some chemical change. Her real reasons are obvious; the fictional reasons which she puts into the mouth of the discoverer are the result of his horrible experiences with the "Frankenstein Monster" which he had created and could not control. "I will not lead you on, unguarded and ardent as I then was, to your destruction and infallible misery."

The imaginations of later writers were stimulated by *Frankenstein* to use the theme of the creation of life. The Monster is the ancestor of many synthetic human beings and robots. But what is more significant, however questionable the science, Mary had added a useful and pointed phrase to the English vocabulary. In an ironic sense it is easy to apply it to many of the recent inventions and discoveries of man's mind. Frankenstein's motives were not merely the disinterested motives of pure research: he saw himself as the benefactor of the world, creating a new and happy species and even restoring the dead to life. Instead he had created a monstrosity and brought death to the living. We hear almost daily in this Atomic Age the mourning voice of the scientist speaking the words of Frankenstein: "Alas! I had turned loose into the world a depraved wretch, whose delight was in carnage and misery; had he not murdered my brother?" And the creature used for destruction warns: "You are my creator, but I am your master."

Shelley's Other Scientific Tales

Frankenstein did not exhaust Mary's use of ancient alchemy and contemporary science. She wrote a short story, "The Mortal Immortal," on the theme of [German magician and alchemist] Cornelius Agripa's elixir of life. She told another "tale of impious tempting of Providence," in which the exchange of souls between two persons is effected by a mingling of their blood; "Transformation" is a short story of magic and presumption whose satisfactory denouement and impeccable moral won it entrance into the pages of the "splendid annuals." She left in manuscript and incomplete a story of an ancient Roman brought back to life in modern Italy. In her other novel of pure imagination, *The Last Man*, she speculated on the future progress in medicine, scientific farming, machinery, and aviation which determined her picture of a happy society nearly three centuries after her time.

Mary Shelley's Knowledge of Science Was Limited

Radu Florescu

Radu Florescu has served as professor of history at Boston College. He is the author of books on Romania, Dracula, *and* Frankenstein.

According to Florescu in this viewpoint, although scientific discovery was all around Mary Shelley in the early nineteenth century and her companions—particularly her husband, Percy Bysshe Shelley, and Lord Byron's personal physician, Dr. John Polidori—displayed a profound interest in science, it seems likely that she had little more than a superficial understanding of the sciences. Florescu claims that two major influences on Shelley's creation of the monster in Frankenstein *were the scientist Sir Humphry Davy and the physician Erasmus Darwin. Yet the novel has no specific references to their work. Instead, Florescu argues, the most intriguing element in the novel—the creation of life—is described in a mere paragraph, and the novel generally displays a dearth of genuine scientific elements.*

The theme of the creation of an artificial man was not new to Mary Shelley; it has ancient origins. The creation of man by divine intervention can be traced to the myth of Prometheus, or to that of Pygmalion, or even to the older Hebrew legends of the Golem. Many early alchemists like [Renaissance alchemist] Paracelsus, [magician and alchemist Cornelius] Agrippa, [theologian and physiologist] Albertus Magnus, and even [German alchemist] Konrad Dippel, had attempted in their nefarious pursuits to play God by creating humans in test tubes, by the distillation of blood, or by other complicated occult practices. The early scientists of the eighteenth and early nineteenth centuries, like Luigi Galvani, Count Volta, and Benjamin Franklin, all of whom experimented with the powers of electricity, were in their own way, working with the power to infuse the spark of life into inanimate matter. Their experiments, coupled with the manufacture and perfection during Mary's time of mechanical men, or androids, by such men as Vaucanson and Jaquet-Droz reinforced the scientific and occult environment in which Mary was writing her novel. . . .

How deeply was Mary Shelley really versed in such subjects as physics, chemistry, biology, medicine, anatomy, physiology, and psychology? Did she really understand [English physician William] Harvey's theory of the circulation of the blood, the manner in which the retina could be attached to the eye, or the latest medical use of the recently discovered power of electricity? The answers to these questions will enable us to determine whether, in fact, *Frankenstein* can legitimately be described as a genuine work of science fiction—in the genre of a [nineteenth-century science fiction author] Jules Verne, or whether it belongs to a more occult tradition.

Frankenstein's Scarcity of Genuine Science

Genuine scientific elements are scarce in the novel. In the Preface to the first edition and in the Introduction to the 1831 edition, Mary and [husband Percy Bysshe] Shelley imply at least some actual scientific research in the statement: "The event on which this fiction is founded has been supposed by Dr. [Erasmus] Darwin and some of the physiological writers of Germany, as not of impossible occurrence." In the Introduction to the 1831 edition Mary states: "They talked of the experiments of Dr. Darwin (I speak not of what the Doctor really did, or said that he did, but as more to my purpose, of what *was then spoken of as having been done by him* [author's italics]), who preserved a piece of vermicelli [pasta] in a glass case, till, by some means it began to move with voluntary motion." (This seems to be an oblique and unscientific statement, since scientists do not conduct their experiments on the basis of hearsay.) Mary continues, "Not thus, after all, would life be given. Perhaps a corpse could be re-animated: galvanism had given token of such things: perhaps the component parts of a creature might be manufactured, brought together, and endued with vital warmth." This statement might lead the reader to suspect some detailed analysis of the use of the powers of electricity in stimulating life, in line with the latest experiments of Volta, Galvani, or Darwin, and reflecting the latest nineteenth-century scientific and medical discoveries—but again the reader will be disappointed. In the crucial chapter on the creation of the monster, instead of an elaborate scientific description of the monster's manufacture, Mary simply notes:

> It was on a dreary night of November, that I beheld the accomplishment of my toils. With an anxiety which almost amounted to agony, I collected the instruments of life around me, that I might infuse a spark of being into the lifeless thing that lay at my feet. It was already in the morning: the rain pattered dismally against the panes, and my candle was nearly burnt out, when, by the glimmer of the half-extinguished light, I saw the dull yellow eye of the creature open; it breathed hard, and a convulsive motion agitated its limbs.

No laboratory capturing the elemental powers of the sun or of lightning? No specific reference to the latest discoveries of Erasmus Darwin or Sir Humphry Davy concerning the use of electricity in animating muscles? Even describing the actual construction of the lifeless monster, Mary displays little knowledge of the human anatomy, of the connection of muscles, tissues, arteries, or veins; nor does the chapter reveal any scientific data concerning the details of the human skeleton, the tibia, or the skull. We are left with the explanation that Frankenstein pursued his filthy work in charnel houses. When finally Victor Frankenstein discovers "the principle of life" which he has studied for months, that discovery is revealed in one simple and disappointing sentence: "After days and nights of incredible labour and fatigue, I succeeded in discovering the cause of generation and life; nay, more, I became capable of bestowing animation upon lifeless matter." What explains Mary's extraordinary reticence in revealing any detail that might lead the reader to infer a genuine knowledge of science and medicine? Was it due to a sense of delicacy, a desire not to shock the moral and religious scruples of her sensitive early nineteenth-century readers? Or to the ill-digested nature of the knowledge which she had gathered from others and which she was too timid to reveal?

The Scientific Sources

If Mary's novel has any claim to genuine science fiction, it must rest on the scientific environment of the eighteenth and nineteenth centuries and the discoveries in physics, biology, chemistry, medicine, and surgery. M.K. Joseph states in his Introduction [to his edition of *Frankenstein*] that Mary linked the myth of Prometheus with "certain current scientific theories which suggested that the 'divine spark' of life might be electrical or quasi-electrical in nature." Who were the major scientists of the time that influenced Mary's creation?

Sir Humphry Davy. Within [Mary's father] William Godwin's circle of friends there was a remarkable scientist, Sir Humphry Davy (1778–1829), whose career in many respects parallels that of Konrad Dippel. Davy's career began in natural philosophy and metaphysics, and gradually shifted to the study of mathematics. At the age of nineteen, he began to study chemistry, being particularly interested in the use of chemical compounds and gases for curing disease, and at the age of 22, when Mary was barely 9 years old, Davy was appointed to the prestigious Chemistry Lectureship at the Royal Institute of

Sir Humphry Davy, a prominent scientist who focused on chemical physiology, influenced Mary Shelley's creation of Frankenstein's monster. © Interfoto/Alamy.

London and won universal acclaim for a lecture he delivered in 1806, and subsequently published, an article entitled "On the chemical effects of electricity" which won him a prize from the French Institute. (Quite a remarkable distinction in view of the fact that England and France were at war at the time.) His health weakened as a result of his endeavors, Davy returned to Geneva in 1826 and was one of the few Englishmen in whose honor the Swiss government gave a public funeral on May 29th, 1829. At the time Davy was barely aged 51. Appropriately enough he was buried at the cemetery of Plainpalais [Switzerland], where the monster committed his first crime. From her journal it is apparent that Mary started reading Davy's *Elements of Chemical Philosophy* (1812) on October 28, 1816, although she refers to it as "Introduction to Davy's Chemistry." At the time Mary was at Great Marlow and was busy writing *Frankenstein*. Davy's book was extolled earlier in the *Quarterly Review*, which Mary read: "It had most assuredly fallen to the lot of no one individual to contribute to the progress of chemical knowledge by discoveries so numerous and important as those that have been made by Sir H. Davy ... we do not hesitate to rank his researches as more splendidly successful than any which have before illustrated the physical sciences." The reviewer added that the author's "discovery relating to electricity" is paramount to that of Franklin and Volta.

As a prelude to Davy, Mary's attention had been riveted to the power of electricity during the lightning storms over Lake Léman [now Geneva]. [Poet Lord] Byron claimed that he had witnessed a dead tree spring to life when hit by lightning, and the conversations at [his villa] Diodati may have revolved around the electrical discoveries of the time—those of Benjamin Franklin (1706–1790), who, with the aid of his metal and silk kites, flown during thunderstorms, had conclusively proven that lightning *is* electricity. One of Mary and Shelley's favorite sports was flying balloons over the lake. Were they performing experiments of this kind? Shelley's fascination with the electrical powers of the galvanic battery when he was at Eton has been well-documented thus far. Although we do not know for sure that Mary read Volney's *Ruins of Empire*, the monster mentions having read it. Indeed, Volney ponders whether electricity might not be the fundamental principle in the universe: "the more I consider what the ancients under-stood by ether or spirit, and what the Indians call *akache*, the stronger do I find the analogy between it and the electrical fluid."

The manner in which Luigi Galvani (1737–1798) pro-duced a continuous flow of electricity has been related many times, as has the episode of the frog's legs, where Galvani's wife happened to notice the convulsive movements produced in a skinned frog when the nerves in the leg were accidentally touched by a scalpel lying on the table that had become charged by contact with an adjoining electrical machine. She communicated her fascination to her husband whose experi-ments concluded that the source of electricity lay in the nerve and that the metals simply acted as conductors. This theory was later contradicted by Count Alessandro Volta (1745–1827) of the University of Pavia, creator of the Voltaic cell and in-ventor of the first electric battery, who contended that the electrical power lay in the metals themselves.

The Source and Science of Life

Erasmus Darwin. Erasmus Darwin (1731–1802), grandfather of Charles Darwin (the most famous theoretician of the evo-lutionary theory of man and the author of *The Origin of Species*), was an English physician, physiologist, psychologist, chemist, geographer, meteorologist, engineer, botanist, and poet. Reference to the work of this famous scientist in both the Preface to the 1818 edition, and the Introduction to the 1831 edition is highly significant. Both Mary and Shelley had every reason to read the works of this extraordinary physician. His *Zoonomia, or the laws of organic life* (1794–1796) was called the "most original book ever written by man." But in addition the Shelleys had a far more personal connection with Darwin. Being an atheist, he shared Mary's and Shelley's skep-ticism about the [biblical] Genesis interpretation of the ori-gins of man (he gave the first somewhat timid impulse to his grandson's evolutionary theory); like Mary and Shelley, Darwin was a romantic, a free thinker, and a rebel against eighteenth-century morality; he was sympathetic to [Mary Shelley's mother] Mary Wollstonecraft's practice of free love; like Mary and Shelley, Darwin was an artful mechanic and engineer; he was interested in automatons and had perfected all kinds of robots, speaking machines, copying machines, and somewhat irreverently he had even manufactured a "speaking priest." Like the Shelleys, he was also a lover of plants who believed with Peter Tompkins and Christopher Bird [authors of *The Secret Life of Plants*] that plants have an existence of their own, akin to man. He also had had the unique opportunity of meeting [French Romantic philosopher] Jean Jacques Rousseau in 1776; he was a friend of Mary Wollstonecraft's publisher Johnson, of Priestly, and of other members of Godwin's intimate Skinner Street Circle. In fact, Godwin had called on Erasmus Darwin in 1797, some two months before Mary Wollstonecraft died. At the time Darwin was away at Shrewsbury, and so the two great radical thinkers of the time did not meet. Godwin later regretted that he did not wait for the return of "so extraordinary a man, so truly a phenomenon."

Darwin was undoubtedly one of the most artful medical practitioners of the eighteenth century. Like [Byron's personal physician, John] Polidori, he had obtained his medical diploma from the prestigious University of Edinburgh. He believed in the psychic origin and treatment of most diseases, and had risked his family's life by experimenting with a measles inoculation. Like Galvani, Volta, Franklin, and Davy, Darwin had also seen the future importance of electricity in curing disease, in stimulating paralyzed muscles by electric shock at a time when the medical practice considered this new power a mere toy. In the *Botanical Garden* he records that: "The temporary motion of a paralytic limb is likewise caused by passing the electric shock through it; which would seem to indicate some analogy between the electric fluid and the nervous fluid, which is separated from the blood by the brain, and thence diffused along the nerves for the purpose of motion and sensation."

There can be no question of Darwin's influence, particularly on [Percy] Shelley, who was enthused by his theory of the possible reanimation of life by the use of electricity. The poet had read Darwin's books: *The Botanic Garden* (1791), the *Temple of Nature* (1804), and *Zoonomia, or the laws of organic life* (1794–96) as early as 1811, and inevitably communicated his enthusiasm to Mary, who learned most of Darwin's theories from Shelley (there is no evidence in her journal that she actually read his books, a difficult task for a non-scientist). [Desmond] King-Hele, one of Darwin's biographers, may be exaggerating when he says that "Darwin stands, then, as a father-figure over this first and most famous work of science fiction."

Bold Scientific Experiments

Theories of the spontaneous regeneration of matter were also popular during Mary's time, and it is possible that her reference in the 1818 Preface to the animation of man as "not of impossible occurrence" referred to the work of a German doctor, George Frank von Frankenau (the name is uncannily close to Frankenstein), who was also ennobled by Emperor Leopold for his work, and who might be called the father of the science of *Palingenetics*—or the science of successive rebirths. Von Frankenau, who studied the regeneration of plants and animals, used their respective ashes in attempting to reproduce microorganisms. His writings may have incited other scientists, such as the Englishman John Turberville Needham (1713–1781), who, by infusing animal and vegetable substances, believed that putrefactions were capable of producing worm-like microorganisms. Needham also experimented with the regeneration of eels.

The eighteenth century witnessed a number of far bolder experiments of this nature, among them those of René Antoine Réaumur (1683–1757), who studied the regeneration of lost parts of crustaceans. Assuredly the most publicized experiment of this nature was conducted by Abraham Trembley (1700–1784), who was able to demonstrate that water hydra, when cut into pieces, could regenerate "into as many complete new polyps as there were severed portions of the original one." Charles Bonnet (1720–1793), a Swiss naturalist and philosopher who was also conducting studies on water hydras and other sea animals who had lost some membrane, proved convincingly that their lost parts could be reproduced by fusion and regeneration. Elected a member of the Royal Society in 1743, he obtained fame with his eight-volume work on natural history and philosophy (1779–83), and in particular for his work *Palingenetic Philosophy*, in which he enunciated a theory on the immortality of all forms of life. Other studies of animal or vegetable regeneration occurred in France by people such as [anatomist Marie-François-Xavier] Bichat (1771–1802), whose *Physiological Studies on Life and Death* was published in 1802.

Mary's Limited Scientific Knowledge

How much science did Mary really understand? Her balloon-flying experiments notwithstanding, the chances are that her mind was of a more literary than scientific bent. She had probably a very slim grasp of the theories expounded by Erasmus Darwin, Sir Humphry Davy, or the "physiological writers" of Germany. For [Percy] Shelley it was different, however; in spite of his penchant for the occult, or perhaps because of it, he was fascinated by chemistry and biology, as his early experiments at Eton and later have clearly demonstrated. Besides, Shelley had briefly studied medicine in London. Dr. John Polidori was also a scientist, having trained at one of the best medical schools in England, the University of Edinburgh.

We know that Polidori had had ample opportunity, during the week that Byron and Shelley were on the *Tour du Lac* [tour of the lake, Geneva, in 1816] to elaborate on the conversation of "first principles" for Mary. M.K. Joseph, in his Introduction, suggests that Victor Frankenstein's change of emphasis from alchemy to chemistry and electricity surely suggests the lesser influence of Godwin's occultism and the greater influence of Shelley and Polidori, whose interests in electricity made it, rather than alchemy, the animating force for the monster.

Frankenstein
and Bioethics

Frankenstein Is an Early Research Ethics Text

Hugh Davies

Hugh Davies is a consultant pediatrician working at the Oxford Radcliffe Hospital and research ethics adviser at the National Research Ethics Service in London, England.

In the following viewpoint Davies observes that Frankenstein has traditionally been read as a warning that scientific experimentation leads inevitably to tragedy. While the dangers of science certainly form a theme of the story, a more balanced view of the novel finds that Mary Shelley is exploring the potential for good as well as for evil, explains Davies. Shelley admired scientific exploration, and it took a special set of circumstances in the novel for Victor Frankenstein's work to fail. In particular, the author asserts, Frankenstein worked completely alone, divorced himself from family and society, and hid his labors from oversight by any authorities. Even today outside scrutiny of medical experimentation is a must; scientists such as Frankenstein would be doomed to failure in any era. Thus, Davies argues, the novel functions as an early text on research ethics that can be valuable to contemporary researchers.

Mary Shelley conceived the idea for and started writing *Frankenstein* in 1816 and it was first published in 1818. In its historical context, the earlier 17th and 18th centuries had seen the early signs of the rise of science and experimentation. [English philosopher] Francis Bacon (1561–1626) had laid the theoretical foundations in his "Great Instauration" and scientists such as [Robert] Boyle, [Sir Isaac] Newton, and

Hugh Davies, "Can Mary Shelley's *Frankenstein* Be Read as an Early Research Ethics Text?" *Journal of Medical Ethics; Medical Humanities*, vol. 30, 2004, pp. 32–35. Copyright © 2004 British Medical Association. Reproduced by permission of the BMJ Publishing Group Ltd.

[Robert] Hooke developed the experimental methods. Sir Robert Talbor, a 17th-century apothecary [pharmacist] and one of the key figures in developing the use of quinine to treat fevers, underlined this: "the most plausible reasons unless backed by some demonstrable experiments seem but suppositions or conjectures".

Medical Experimentation in Shelley's Time

The 18th century saw the continued construction of foundations upon which all subsequent medical experimentation has been built. [English writer] Lady Mary Montagu promoted smallpox vaccination; its proponents experimented on prisoners to study its efficacy, and James Jurin, the secretary of the Royal Society [a British scientific organization], developed mathematical proof of this in the face of ecclesiastical opposition. Many of the modern concepts of therapeutic trials were described although not widely accepted. Empirical observation through experimentation was starting to be recognised as the tool that allowed ascertainment of fact and truth. An account of [18th-century physician] Dr Bianchini's experiments on "Le Medicin Electrique", reported to the Royal Society explains that "The experiments were made by Dr Bianchini assisted by several curious and learned men . . . who not being able to separate what was true . . . determined to be guided by their own experiments and it was by this most troublesome though of all the others the most sure way, that they have learned to reject a great number of what have been published as facts."

Similarly, [English naturalist] Henry Baker's report to the Royal Society, describing [French physicist] Abbe Nollet's experiments, outlined the need for comparative studies and that "treatment should not be condemned without a fair trial" and a Belgian doctor, Professor Lambergen, describing the use of deadly nightshade for the treatment of breast cancer wrote "Administration of this plant certainly merits the attention of the medical profession; and surely one may add entitles the medicine to future trials . . . nevertheless the most efficacious medicines are such if its efficacy by repeated trials be approved."

In the mid 18th century [Scottish physician] James Lind conducted the first controlled trial to establish a cure for scurvy and his *Treatise on the Scurvy* contains what could be seen in modern terminology as the first "review of the current literature" prior to a clinical trial.

Shelley's Motives for Writing *Frankenstein*

Mary Shelley certainly knew of experiments with electricity ("galvanism"), probably through her parents [William Godwin and Mary Wollstonecraft], whose acquaintances included many experimentalists and her husband [Percy Bysshe Shelley] who had himself conducted his own experiments. Her introduction to the 1831 edition gives support: "perhaps a corpse would be re-animated; galvanism had given token of such things . . . perhaps the component parts of a creature might be manufactured . . . and endued with vital warmth."

Her motives for writing *Frankenstein* are more difficult to define. In her introduction to the 1831 edition she writes that she wanted her work to

> . . . speak to the mysterious fears of our nature and awaken thrilling horror—one to make the reader dread to look round. If I did not accomplish these things, my ghost story would be unworthy of its name . . .

This is supported by the events around the creation of the story in Geneva. During their stay, Lord Byron had, one evening, challenged his companions Percy Shelley, James [Polidori], and Mary Shelley to create and relate a ghost story.

In addition to this desire to instil fear, she also seemed to want to write a cautionary tale, warning of the consequences of creating human life:

> . . . frightful would be the effect of any human endeavour to mock the stupendous mechanism of the creator . . .

The 1818 preface, written by Percy Bysshe Shelley, indicates a deeper purpose. He wrote that the story recommends itself as it ". . . affords a point of view on the imagination for the delineating of human passions more comprehensive and commanding than any which the ordinary relations of existing events can yield . . ." and that ". . . I am by no means indifferent to the manner in which . . . moral tendencies (that) exist in the sentiments of characters shall affect the reader . . ."

Such a work must inevitably explore the moral issues consequent upon its creation. What is interesting is that despite Mary Shelley's expressed abhorrence of assuming divine powers and creating human life, the novel is far from an outright condemnation of [Victor] Frankenstein, the creator of the monster, or of his actions. We find a surprisingly balanced judgement. The possibilities and dangers of science are recognised as are the strengths and frailties of human beings.

If, therefore, this evidence indicates that the novel *Frankenstein* is based in the science of its day, what can be learnt of relevance to those undertaking ethical review of such research today?

The Value of Scientific Research

Frankenstein's story as told to [character Robert] Walton is a cautionary tale, but within this there is a clear appreciation of the power of scientific experimentation.

The principal human characters, Robert Walton and Victor Frankenstein recognise the potential of knowledge derived from experiment. The novel starts with letters from the explorer Robert Walton to his sister Margaret in which he describes how he himself had used science: "I often worked harder . . . and devoted my nights to the study of mathematics, the theory of medicine, and those branches of physical science from which a naval adventure might derive the greatest practical advantage."

Later Frankenstein expresses a similar view, "... that a modern system of science had been introduced, which possessed much greater powers, real and practical ...", and praises the "wonderful discoveries of the modern philosophers."

Others reiterate this view. Waldeman, one of Frankenstein's professors, describes science's potential:

> Modern masters ... have performed miracles. They penetrate into the recesses of nature and show how she works ... they have acquired new and almost unlimited powers.

Few would dispute this view now and this idea has wide support. It is self evident that medical treatments have improved in recent centuries and that these developments are founded upon experimentation. Supporting this view, the introduction to the Governance Arrangements for Research Ethics Committees (GAfREC) in the United Kingdom [UK] contains the statement "Research is essential to the successful promotion and protection of health and social care."

Any body undertaking review of medical research now must take this into consideration but in Mary Shelley's time this thesis was more speculative. There was little practical evidence to support the argument. It was not evident that medicine or science had improved any aspect of life at the start of the 18th century. Crude measurements such as life expectancy had not improved and few therapeutic advances had been made. The views expressed by Shelley's characters were ahead of their time and prophetic.

Scientific Experimentation Can Harm

To counterbalance this potential benefit, Frankenstein also recognises the seductive excitement of scientific discovery. He describes his feelings as the "secrets of nature were revealed" to him: "Gladness akin to rapture, as they were unfolded to me" and his later discovery "From the midst [of] this darkness a sudden light broke upon me—a light so brilliant and won-drous" and "The astonishment soon gave place to delight and rapture."

The book continues to develop how this can lead to a darker side of science. Frankenstein warned Walton to "Learn from me how dangerous is the acquirement of knowledge" and explained its seductive power: "None but those who have experienced them can conceive the enticements of science."

In modern times, we have learnt that in the quest for knowledge, experiments can seriously harm subjects. Some of the women recruited by [German physician Albert] Neisser into his experiments to develop an antisyphilis serum con-tracted the disease themselves. Many in the concentration camps were brutally killed in Nazi experiments. Poor African Americans were observed and treatment withheld as they de-veloped syphilis in the Tuskegee experiment and children ad-mitted to the Willowbrook unit in New York State were delib-erately infected with hepatitis A. The novel *Frankenstein* provides insight as to how and why some scientists, enticed by scientific endeavours and their successes, can lose their moral perspective.

Scientists Are Not a Species Apart

The description of Victor Frankenstein is far from his being evil, indeed the very opposite: we read of a compassionate and learned man. Walton's portrait stands as testament:

> Sometimes I have endeavoured to discover what quality he possesses that elevates him so immeasurably above any other person I ever knew ... intuitive discernment ... never fail-ing power of judgement.

We also find evidence of Frankenstein's moral values. He admits to doubts about his purpose: "I doubted at first whether I should attempt the creation ...", and he also dem-onstrates personal insight into his character: "My imagination was too much exalted by my first success."

When he met the monster again, he first agreed to create a companion but finally stood firm and refused. He understood the conflicting moral duties to his family and the being he created, but saw that those to his family were greater. It was only with great anguish after wrestling with his conscience that he denied the monster a companion.

The Danger of Separating Scientist and Society

Pursuing his experiments, Frankenstein worked alone and was ultimately seduced by science and his early experimental successes. Yet this weakness is far from the marker of an evil personality, a view attested to by Walton. We see a scientist working alone, divorced from family and society. His only contact seemed to be with other scientists. These self imposed privations at university ultimately led to illness and breakdown. "Natural philosophy . . . became nearly my sole occupation."

His progress and single minded dedication were reinforced by the approbation of the only people he met: "I had made some discoveries, which procured me great esteem and admiration at the university"; and ultimately he lost moral perspective, was seduced and finally captured by science: "The professors' words enounced to destroy me . . . my soul was gripped by a palpable enemy."

> During my first experiment a kind of frenzy had blinded me to the horror of employment; my mind was intently fixed on the consummation of my labour and my eyes shut to the horror of my proceedings.

The potential of science and his own early success first motivated and then seduced Frankenstein. The choice of words is deliberate. The *Oxford English Dictionary* defines motivation as "that which moves a person to act" in contrast to seduction as "that which persuades to leave duty or allegiance to beguile to do something wrong." Frankenstein was clearly "seduced".

Clearly he ultimately neglected his duties and forgot his allegiances to his family and society.

There are resonances with William Godwin's (Mary Shelley's father) views and with views current in the community of research reviewers, that scientist and society must work together. Those who met the monster did not appreciate his initial benevolence; they obviously knew nothing of the experiments or the monster's personal tragedy. "I am malicious because I am miserable. Am I not shunned and hated by all mankind." Godwin wrote:

> Knowledge, and the enlargement of intellect are poor, when unmixed with sentiments of benevolence and sympathy ... and science and abstraction will soon become cold, unless they derive new attractions from ideas of society.

In modern guidance to institutional review boards (IRBs) and research ethics committees (RECs), Food and Drug Administration regulations, International Commission on Harmonisation—Good Clinical Practice, and GAfREC [Governance Arrangements for Research Ethics Committees] require researchers and IRBs/RECs, as one of society's representatives in the debate on medical research, to collaborate with researchers in the protection of research subjects.

> The protection of research participants is best served by close co-operation and efficient communication amongst all who share responsibility ... participants, research funders, sponsors and employers.

Mary Shelley's novel gives us a hideous insight into the consequences of separation of scientist and society. In our current model the IRB/REC is one of the key representatives of society. There is further support for this collaboration in the UK. GAfREC proposes that the REC role must include the facilitation of ethical research, a task impossible without close collaboration between researcher and reviewer.

The Central Issue of the Character of the Researcher

Tragedy rests upon a susceptible but not evil personality, with common human frailties. I believe we can find early clues in the description of Frankenstein's conversations with his "cousin", Elizabeth. She seemed to delight in nature while he earnestly sought the causes: "I was capable of a more intense application," suggesting that he could more easily lose human perspective when applying himself to study. We also read of his intense ambitions developing from his reading of science: "So much has been done, far more will I achieve: treading in the steps already marked, I will pioneer a new way, explore unknown powers, and unfold to the world the deepest mysteries of creation" which interestingly he recognised: "From my infancy I was imbued with high hopes and a lofty ambition."

Frankenstein, himself, attributes events to "enthusiastic madness" and maintains he was not to be blamed: "During these last days I have been occupied in examining my past conduct: nor do I find it blameable. In a fit of enthusiastic madness I created a rational creature." . . .

Whatever her ultimate reasons and personal beliefs, Mary Shelley provides us with a novel that explores the problems consequent upon medical experimentation. The question she addresses could be succinctly framed: "What would happen if a scientist undertook an experiment to create human life?"

Nowadays IRBs and RECs undertake their work with a similar question. We are asked to consider, "What would happen if the scientist before us undertook this research proposal? Would the consequences be morally and ethically acceptable?"

Shelley's Victor Frankenstein Was Modeled After an Eccentric Physician

Christopher Goulding

Christopher Goulding is an English teacher at the Royal Grammar School in Newcastle upon Tyne, England. He has written extensively on Percy Bysshe Shelley and other English Romantic writers.

Goulding writes in the following selection that because Frankenstein *is such a powerful moral and philosophical tale, few attempts have been made to trace the characters back to their biographical originals. Goulding sees a prototype for Victor Frankenstein in the Scottish physician James Lind, who was a friend and mentor of Mary Shelley's poet husband, Percy. Lind's scientific interests parallel those of the novel's protagonist. His fascination with animal electricity led him to perform experiments similar to those of Luigi Galvani, the Italian physicist who sent charges of electrical current through dead frogs. Lind's speculation about the reanimation of dead bodies may have sparked the creative interest of Percy, and through him Mary, asserts Goulding, and inspired her creation of Frankenstein's monster.*

Mary Shelley's novel *Frankenstein* has become one of the most analysed literary texts of the modern age. Its central theme provides a metaphor conducive to almost limitless reinterpretation, drawn by different readings into the service of numerous ideologies including marxist economics, radical feminism, green politics, and, most recently, genetics and biotechnology.

Christopher Goulding, "The Real Dr. Frankenstein?" *Journal of the Royal Society of Medicine*, vol. 95, May 2002, pp. 257–59. Reproduced by permission.

As Mary Shelley's concerns clearly lie with the moral and sociological implications of her story, attempts to identify likely origins for the scientific elements of the story have attracted less attention, and generally refer only to the contemporaneous sources easily available to the educated public. Nevertheless, doubts exist concerning Mary Shelley's degree of specific interest in, or knowledge of, scientific subjects. Accordingly, the level of influence exerted in this field by her husband, the poet Percy Bysshe Shelley, also remains open to debate. He maintained a keen interest in the world of natural philosophy, and many critics have noted the significance of the references to 'Dr [Erasmus] Darwin and some of the physiological writers of Germany' in the novel's Preface, which was written by him. But a closer examination of the medical themes running throughout the novel strongly suggests a more obscure influence at work, arising from Percy Shelley's friendship with a Scots doctor whilst he was still a schoolboy at Eton.

An Alchemist in Windsor

During his last two years at Eton in 1809–1810, Percy Shelley became the friend of an elderly gentleman who was one of several people approved by the school as suitable mentors for the boys. Dr James Lind MD FRS [Fellow of the Royal Society] (1736–1812) was a widower living in semi-retirement at nearby Windsor. Born and educated in Edinburgh, he had travelled extensively as a ship's surgeon to Africa, India, and China. Lind was also an accomplished astronomer and geologist, and had accompanied Sir Joseph Banks of the Royal Society on a scientific expedition to Iceland in 1772. This James Lind is not to be confused with his more famous cousin and namesake (1716–1794), the 'father of nautical medicine' and author of *A Treatise on the Scurvy*.

To polite society in Windsor, Lind appeared something of an eccentric. This image was later confirmed by his son Alexander, who vividly evoked the alchemic appearance of his father's study in the family home: 'There were telescopes, Galvanic Batteries, Daggers, Electrical Machines, and all the divers apparatus which a philosopher is supposed to possess'.

Lind was, in fact, a highly knowledgeable natural philosopher with a keen interest in the latest developments in every emerging field of science that was later to attract the young poet Shelley. He was a friend, acquaintance, or correspondent of most of the great names of eighteenth century science, philosophy, and technology, including [American inventor] Benjamin Franklin, [astronomer] William Herschel, [English philosopher] David Hume, [Scottish economist] Adam Smith and [Scottish inventor] James Watt. In Mary Shelley's uncompleted and fragmentary posthumous biography of her husband, she was later to state that at Eton he:

> ... became intimate also with a man whom he never mentioned except in terms of the tenderest respect. This was Dr Lind, a name well known among the professors of medical science ... he has often said ... "I owe that man far—oh! Far more than I owe my father."

[Percy] Shelley's friend [British writer] Thomas Jefferson Hogg noted that Lind 'communicated to Shelley a taste for chemistry and chemical experiments'. Hogg also remarked that in Shelley's rooms at Oxford there was a confusion of clutter: '... An electrical machine, an air pump, the galvanic trough, a solar microscope, and ... a small glass retort above an argand lamp'.

Percy Shelley later immortalized Lind in verse as the character Zonoras, the wise old teacher of Prince Athanase in the eponymously titled poem:

Prince Athanase had one beloved friend

An old, old man, with hair of silver white

And lips where heavenly smiles would hang
and blend

With his wise words; and eyes whose arrowy
light

Shone like the reflex of a thousand minds.

The Shelleys and Science

There can be little doubt that Mary Shelley owed much of
what medical knowledge she had to her husband's abiding interest, as inspired by Lind. Before meeting his wife, the poet
had read such medical works as Thomas Trotter's *A View of
the Nervous Temperament* (1812) and was familiar with the
extensively annotated scientific poetry, expounding the obser-
vations, theories, and predictions of the physician and natural
philosopher Erasmus Darwin. Recent editors of *Frankenstein*
have also noted that Percy Shelley could have been aware of
'the physiological writers of Germany' via his personal physician William Lawrence, who had translated [physician Johann
Friedrich] Blumenbach's *Comparative Anatomy* in 1807.

Mary Shelley's journals painstakingly (though by no means
exhaustively) itemize her husband's systematic reading programme from the date of their elopement in 1814. She also
records an outing with him in London on 28 December that
year to see a public lecture on galvanism and the medicinal
uses of electricity by [French inventor] André-Jacques Gar-
nerin. (Percy Shelley went again the following evening with
another friend, but found the lecture hall closed.)

Recent biography of Mary Shelley has suggested closer
links between the author herself and the purely medical aspects of her novel. These include her possible reading of accounts during 1814 of the restoration to consciousness of a
sailor who had lain in a coma for several months; the doctor
concerned was Henry Cline, whose patient Mary had once
been. Also cited is an entry in Mary's journal for 19 March
1815, shortly after the death of her first baby: 'Dream that my
little baby came to life again—that it had only been cold &
that we rubbed it by the fire & it lived'. Another proposed link

is one between Mary's father, the philosopher William God-win, and Luigi Galvani via a review in March 1800 by two of Godwin's friends, the physicist William Nicholson and the surgeon Anthony Carlisle, of a paper by Volta, who had previously challenged Galvani's theories of 'animal electricity'.

Giving Life to a Haunting Story

Mary Shelley was eighteen years old when she began her story whilst a guest at [poet] Lord Byron's Villa Diodati on the shores of Lake Geneva during the summer of 1816. Some detail of the novel's origins was later to emerge in her introduction to the revised single-volume edition of 1831, where she describes how she was a 'silent listener' to the long philosophical discussions of her husband with Lord Byron:

> 'They talked of the experiments of Dr Darwin ... who preserved a piece of vermicelli [pasta] in a glass case till by some extraordinary means it began to move with a voluntary motion. Not thus, after all, would life be given. Perhaps a corpse would be reanimated; galvanism had given token of such things: perhaps the component parts of a creature might be manufactured, brought together, and endued with vital warmth.'

She then notes how, inspired by the overheard conversations, her imagination contrived the germ of the story:

> 'I saw the pale student of unhallowed arts kneeling beside the thing he had put together. I saw the hideous phantasm of a man stretched out, and then, on the working of some powerful engine, show signs of life and stir with an uneasy half-vital motion.'

In fact, the account in the novel of the creature's creation by Victor Frankenstein provides only the vaguest detail, culminating in a rather subdued account of its awakening:

> 'It was on a dreary night of November, that I beheld the accomplishment of my toils. With an anxiety that almost

amounted to agony, I collected the instruments of life around me, that I might infuse a spark of being into the lifeless thing that lay at my feet. It was already one in the morning; the rain pattered dismally against the panes, and my candle was nearly burnt out, when by the glimmer of the half-extinguished light, I saw the dull yellow eye of the creature open; it breathed hard, and a convulsive motion agitated its limbs.'

But a reassessment of certain other medical themes and quasi-autobiographical events featured throughout *Franken-stein* might now be said to suggest the influence of Lind's character and work, via his pupil Percy Shelley.

Lind in Frankenstein

The description in the novel of Victor Frankenstein's medical studies at the University of Ingolstadt has been recognized as an idealized version of Percy Shelley's scientific education, with the character Waldman, the chemistry lecturer, owing much to Lind. But an examination of Lind's own experiments reveals that he was even closer to the world of Frankenstein than has hitherto been acknowledged. Between 1782 and 1809, Lind maintained a regular correspondence with the London-based Italian physicist Tiberio Cavallo. Cavallo mentions Galvani's experiments on 10 June 1792, the year following publication of Galvani's research. On 11 July he asks Lind: 'Have you made any dead frogs jump like living ones?', and then on 15 August writes: 'I am glad to hear of your success in the new experiments on muscular motion, and earnestly entreat you to prosecute them to the *ne plus ultra* of possible means'.

Lind also corresponded regularly with Sir Joseph Banks, President of the Royal Society. On 28 October 1792 he thanks Banks for supplying frogs that have enabled him and Cavallo to conduct experiments towards 'the unravelling of that extraordinary and as yet inexplicable phenomenon, *Animal*

Electricity'. Lind also notes how, the previous week, he had demonstrated such an experiment to the King, Queen, and other members of the royal family. In the same letter, he tells of a visit some five weeks earlier of Dr Valli of Pisa, who spent a day with Lind demonstrating '. . . a more perfect manner of preparing the frog by which I could employ both Crural nerves at the same time instead of only part of one of them separated from the thigh. The difference was astonishing'.

He then mentions a letter Cavallo had received from Volta, contesting Galvani's theories. In another letter to Banks dated 27 November 1788, written during one of the King's periods of 'insanity', Lind discusses the possibility of treatment by the application of electricity: 'If we may credit the accounts of the state of the Brain of insane persons found upon dissection, I think there is great reason to believe that it may be of service in that disorder and appears to me to merit a fair tryal'.

Running alongside the novel's central plot concerning the creation of a monster are parallel themes addressing contemporary perceptions of the increasingly blurred boundary between life and death. These include an early excerpt where Victor Frankenstein is dragged freezing and emaciated aboard a ship from an ice floe in the Arctic Ocean:

> 'We accordingly brought him back to the deck, and restored him to animation by rubbing him with brandy, and forcing him to swallow a small quantity. As soon as he showed signs of life, we wrapped him up in blankets . . .'

Later, the creature attempts to resuscitate a young girl whose body he has dragged from a river: 'She was senseless; and I endeavoured, by every means in my power, to restore animation. . .'. Such references recall Lind's own medical education in Edinburgh under William Cullen, who was instrumental in the early codification of procedures for the revival of drowned or otherwise asphyxiated persons.

Cullen is, in fact, mentioned within this context in a medical work known to have been ordered by Percy Shelley from his bookseller in July 1812. Robert Thornton's *Medical Extracts* includes a lengthy passage on methods suitable for persons being 'recalled to life' from 'the silent mansions of the tomb', and mentions the theories of Cullen and Boerhaave on the causes of death from asphyxiation by hanging. Interestingly, another Shelley critic has noted that Waldman's assessment in *Frankenstein* of modern philosophers as the successors to the alchemists bears similarities to comments appearing elsewhere in Thornton's book.

A Medical Muse?

The influence of Lind's medical pursuits extends beyond *Frankenstein*, and is most reflected in Percy Shelley's own works. Examples include the likely effect of Lind's interest in forensic medicine as the inspiration for Percy Shelley's creation of perhaps the earliest example of ratiocinative detective drama in his play *The Cenci*.

Notwithstanding Mary Shelley's own literary talent, and her night of inspiration in 1816, we might now give some credit to the time spent six years previously by her husband-to-be in the study of a retired Scots physician in Windsor.

Victor Frankenstein Is Shelley's True Immortal Monster

M.G.H. Bishop

M.G.H. Bishop has practiced in the Department of Dental Radiology at King's College Hospital in London and has published numerous articles about the intersection of ethics, literature, and medicine.

When thinking about the "remaking of man" through transplant surgery, it is wise to keep the lessons of Mary Shelley's novel in mind, according to Bishop. The conditions and companions in Shelley's life at the time of writing inspired a character of monstrous intentions and practices in Victor Frankenstein. Bishop makes a clear distinction between Frankenstein and modern transplant surgeons and supports serious evaluation of the novel for modern ethical questions of creation. Popular culture sustains a link between the dumb, destructive Frankenstein monster and legitimate surgical procedures, he says, but a loyal reading of Shelley's text provides helpful insight into Victor Frankenstein's failures and, by comparison, the love of humanity that characterizes transplant science today.

The serious and important self-examination stimulated in the medical profession by the successful re-making of man through transplant surgery, and now its newest relation gene therapy, is not challenged or trivialized by a look at the most famous of made men, Mary Shelley's Monster, and the creator herself.

M.G.H. Bishop, "The Making and Re-making of Man: 1. Mary Shelley's *Frankenstein*, and Transplant Surgery," *Journal of the Royal Society of Medicine*, vol. 87, December 1994, pp. 749–51. Reproduced by permission.

A Book to Be Taken Seriously

A serious debate does not impose seriousness on literary sources, where any reference to the subject may help form opinion. A witty collection of recipes exists for creating men, published by Margaret Atwood as 'Making a Man', which she starts with the traditional dust-and-water mix of the biblical account before moving on to gingerbread and other materials. Concise and amusing, it is nevertheless thought provoking. A similar example of a useful, but less than serious, account in the Nature versus Nurture debate on what makes a man, may be found in Osbert Sitwell's short story *Triple Fugue* of 1924, which looks at the results of a surgical melding of body parts taking their natures with them.

Mary Shelley's book on the subject of creation, though, stands alone as source material by virtue of its lasting influence on public thought, and because of the time and circumstance of its writing. It should be taken seriously, for it seems very likely that transplant and eugenic aspects of medical research and surgical practice will forever be associated in the popular press with her novel *Frankenstein, or the Modern Prometheus.*

For medicine to be linked with this fine work, which Shelley published in 1818, is by itself no problem. It is the way in which the references are made that is worth considering with care, and such careful study is the aim of this paper.

The Novelist's Environment

The story of the Shelleys' joint lives, from their first brief meeting in 1812 until [Mary's husband] Percy Bysshe Shelley drowned at sea off the Italian coast 10 years later, is a turbulent one, eclipsing with its deaths and betrayals the agonies of their literary creatures, Prometheus the Titan [the subject of Percy Shelley's *Prometheus Unbound*], and the Modern Prometheus, Frankenstein. Still, it would be unwise to take the simplistic view that the Shelleys were writing when themselves tormented by grief, guilt or remorse, for they were certainly up to leading an astonishingly rackety life. They had lived together on the continent and in England since 1814, when Shelley eloped to the continent with Mary, leaving his pregnant wife Harriet (found drowned in 1816) and his daughter Ianthe. Mary Wollstonecraft Godwin was 18 years old when she started work on *Frankenstein* and was not yet married to Shelley, though she had already in 1815 borne him one daughter who had died, and a son (William, who died in 1819) a few months earlier in 1816. The story grew out of what was almost a party game on a damp holiday in Switzerland, a holiday dogged not just by poor weather, but by personality clashes in a group which included [poet Lord] Byron, his besotted inamorata 'Claire' (Mary's stepsister Jane Clairmont), and Dr John Polidori, Byron's personal physician and travelling companion. . . .

It is a source for wonder that an 18-year-old girl could come by the knowledge and ability to write as she did, and that in the chaos of her life she could find the strength of purpose to see the book through to publication. Her achievement was very great, for Mary Godwin could not go to Wycombe Abbey or St Paul's School for Girls, or any other academy for young ladies, for they did not exist. Her breadth of education instead derived from a fierce determination to learn, first from her father William Godwin and his circle, and then from Shelley and his friends, and by reading what was available. She knew Latin, French, and Italian, and some Greek. Even at that age she must have been formidable, and later in life she became more so. When she was 15, her father described her as

> Singularly bold, somewhat imperious, and active of mind. Her desire for knowledge is great, and her perseverance in everything she undertakes almost invincible.

Models for the Scientist

Her model for [Victor] Frankenstein can only be guessed at. Various suggestions have been made, the important one for [this viewpoint] being that Shelley himself provided the intellectual model, surely the saddest suggestion if Mary already had such an insight into his character, insight which must have come sooner or later to such an intelligence as hers. Dr Polidori, half Italian, half English, educated at Ampleforth and Edinburgh, and qualifying in medicine aged 19 (in 1815) is another possible source, and her father William Godwin could hardly fail to be in there somewhere.

Such detailed speculation is unnecessary. In effect, for his form and speech, Mary Shelley assembled Victor Frankenstein out of all the bits and pieces of the living men that she found lying about in her life, and grafted on more odds and ends retrieved from the 'charnel houses and graveyards' of books she had read. In her case it was a books' graveyard of Highgate Cemetery proportions in which was buried, amongst many others, [French author] Madame de Genlis' *Pygmalion et Galatée*, [German magician and theologian] Cornelius Agrippa, [Renaissance physician] Paracelsus, [German physiologist and philosopher] Albertus Magnus, [English physician] Erasmus Darwin, [Homer's classical epic poem] the *Iliad*, [English poet John] Milton and [Swiss political philosopher] J-J Rousseau, and [English playwright William] Shakespeare. Also there was [English writer] Samuel Richardson, whose idea of writing *Clarissa Harlowe* as a series of letters may have given Mary Shelley the form for her novel, a series of letters from Captain Walton, an Englishman, to his sister.

Frankenstein the Scientist

Having assembled the parts, she then infused the 'man' with life, to such good effect that interest in him has not died since. Frankenstein is thus as much a monster as The Monster, and his life and death as recorded in the book should not be overshadowed by the 'life' and fate, suggested but unspecified, of the latter, certainly the medical reader should concentrate on Frankenstein, for it is with Frankenstein and not the Monster itself that the profession is identified in the public mind.

As each new film of the book is produced, it is interesting to see whether it portrays the 'Doctor' or the 'Scientist'. As he dropped out before completing his studies, we do not know which path he might have taken, but it seems likely that, like Doctor Faustus [the character in Christopher Marlowe's play who sells his soul to the devil], he would not have qualified as a medical doctor. His studies today would probably have led to a PhD, for he studied natural philosophy, anatomy, and chemistry. The *aequanimitas* [evenness of mind or temper] so central to the training of the medical man was not part of his training, and it is by contrast rather than by emulation that the medical man can learn from him. Whatever a new film does for *Frankenstein*, it will do a service if it removes from our consciousness the poor stitching and bolts of previous Monsters, the electric shocks (not in the book) and other accretions of images derived from a thousand and one previous films, comics, imitations and parodies. A film giving us a faithful rendering of the original text, and correcting some of these images, for the shambling doltish figure of the monster of popular imagery can not be found in the sensitive emotions, quick intelligence and physical abilities of the monster of the book, is important. The man is diminished if his creation does not excite our belief and pity as well as our deep fears.

The Novel's Forgotten Mythological Link

The original writer and readers of the novel would not have had our problems. For them it was a completely different work from the one picked up by a modern reader. The name Frankenstein would have meant nothing, and they had no image of the monster, but the additional 'Or The Modern

Prometheus' in the title would have been full of meaning, giving them a backcloth against which the actors on the page could move, with their shadows falling on recognizable scenery that few of us now find so familiar.

As a Titan, Prometheus was of that race which according to Ancient Greek legend, issued from the loins of the oldest god Uranus, the sky (the planet was named after him by Herschel, not the Greeks), and the womb of Gaia, the earth. When Prometheus made humankind from clay, and breathed into them life, it was creation from the very substance of his own being, the clay of his grandmother, the air of his grandfather. The chaining of Prometheus to a rock as punishment by Zeus, his liver devoured each day by an eagle or vulture, was punishment not for the creation of mankind, that could be tolerated if man remained an ignorant and powerless lump. It was for stealing fire from the gods and giving it to his creation that he had to suffer, and the poetical term 'Promethean fire' meant the very inspiration and genius of mankind. Mary Shelley's chosen destination for the end of her monster in fire, though we are left uncertain as to whether it met that end, is entirely fitting, as is the death of Frankenstein in an icy waste, physical and mental.

Science Has Done Terrible Things

Mary Shelley's success in exciting empathy explains why the modern medical reader who has been moved by the novel should feel discomfort when seeing the name of Frankenstein associated with transplant surgery, although the distorted versions of the tale of the monster have a function in the long long line of cautionary stories with which folk wisdom is transmitted. It cannot be denied that terrible things have been done in the name of science, and frightening phenomena have needed avoidance or explanation in primitive communities, and the primitive sits on the shoulder of us all. In picking over the bones of medical stories of transplants and distorting them with the convenient flesh of Frankenstein's monster, the gentlemen of the press are but continuing the tradition. Reading of the original reinstates a much more powerful image.

This is the image of a Frankenstein who is left having made his golem or zombie [inhuman creatures of lore], but without even the excuse, however spurious, that Rabbi Löw [creator of the golem] or a voodoo priest might advance that what was made was a biddable hulk to perform an inhuman task, for he had sought to create a man in all or more of the beauty of that being. The nightmare of his position, and the gothic horror of the novel, lies in his instant awareness on seeing the monster, that he had instead placed a human mind within a grotesque and ghastly cage. This image is not comparable with the achievements of the medical profession with transplant surgery.

The Morality of Modern Transplantation Science

Where the medical profession and science are at their nearest to Frankenstein they are still a world away. Science and surgeons between them have created new life in added years through transplant surgery, and thanks to medicine large numbers of people stay young well into ages inconceivable to the Shelleys' generation. This is sometimes achieved with material derived, as was Frankenstein's, from human tissue and the metals and clay of the earth herself. The difference is that this is not the construction by a Frankenstein profession of unnamed monsters, destined to be unloved and rejected. It is love of a whole humanity that drives such professional endeavour and achievement.

The medical man can and should take part in the debate on the ethics of transplantation, and the moralist, the religious and the social scientist will be only a few of the people who will have views to put forward. Ethics defined in this way refine our practice in a profoundly emotive field where the surgeon could be seen as judge and jury when 'brain death' or even more fetal non-viability is concerned in the search for tissue to employ in transplants.

Frankenstein dreamt of superman. Medicine expects more than that: '*Mens sana in corpore sano*', the healthy mind in the healthy body—and has much less chance of being disappointed.

Frankenstein Comments on the Male Construction of Medical Science

H. Bruce Franklin

Cultural historian H. Bruce Franklin has served as professor of English and American studies at Rutgers University. His numerous books include Future Perfect: American Science Fiction of the Nineteenth Century *and* MIA; or, Mythmaking in America.

Franklin casts a critical eye on the medical profession and the birth process in the following viewpoint, observing that as males came to dominate the medical sphere in the thirteenth through seventeenth centuries, they viewed traditional midwives as threatening to their control of health care. Thus women who practiced medical arts were persecuted as witches. Yet when births were attended by midwives, Franklin contends, the mortality rate for birth mothers was far lower than it was in the care of male doctors, who were taught to rely on unscientific measures. Victor Frankenstein attempts to create a new being to banish disease from humanity, but, as Franklin argues, his attempt to eliminate women from the procreative process is another example of medicine, driven by male hubris, that is doomed to failure.

No single book offers more meaningful and complex interconnections between literature and medicine than Mary Shelley's *Frankenstein; or, The Modern Prometheus*—that "first great myth of the industrial age" [according to Brian Aldiss]. One could easily spend an enlightening [college] semester just exploring the paths opened by this novel. Students of course know the myth—and all refer to that college dropout who created the monster as "Doctor" Frankenstein. I ask them why a novel written almost two centuries ago by someone younger than most of them should still permeate our culture. One answer is obvious: [Victor] Frankenstein is the archetypal scientist, who discovers, invents, or unleashes forces that make humanity confront its own creativity in the form of awesome alien powers.

Progress and Problems in Modern Medicine

Frankenstein is a very particular kind of scientist: a man of medicine. He thus tends to embody some of the contradictions of medicine today. We have marvels of medical technology—genetic engineering, magnetic resonance imaging, organ transplants, arthroscopic surgery, in vitro fertilization, cyborg fantasies materializing as body parts are replaced, boundless promises of health and life. But we also have a disintegrating health delivery system; closed and understaffed hospitals; medical dollars and time gobbled up by endless bureaucratic paper pushing; the resurgence of supposedly archaic diseases like tuberculosis; lurking diseases like Ebola; epidemics of AIDS [acquired immune deficiency syndrome], drug addiction, and cancer; and the vortex of (mis)managed care. And if the individual's life *is* extended, where does it end? In the abyss of a nursing home? As an appendage to life-support machinery? Or with the mercies of a Dr. [Jack] Kevorkian [a physician known for helping terminally ill patients commit suicide]?

I try to defer discussion of all this obvious relevance of *Frankenstein* until after my students and I have explored, in detail, three interrelated topics: the novel's strange narrative structure, the history of medicine as a major context of the novel, and the effects of this history on Mary Shelley's life.

Frankenstein and Scientific Medicine

Although written by a woman, *Frankenstein* consists almost entirely of male voices and seems to be all about the lives of male beings. The entire novel is narrated in letters from Robert Walton, the would-be grand global explorer. Inside his narrative is that of Victor Frankenstein. And inside Frankenstein's narrative is that of his creature. Women are thus presented as the objects of male perception, desires, and fears, and the main female character's primary role is that of victim. But since the letters are all addressed to Walton's sister, Margaret Saville (whose initials happen to be those of the author), the implied listener to these male voices, though silent, is a female consciousness.

Frankenstein appeared during a crucial period in the emergence of what is called "Western," or "scientific," or "modern" medicine, as if these terms are interchangeable and as if all other systems of medicine are merely "alternative." Here we find vital connections between the narrative of the novel, so thoroughly dominated by male voices, and the history of medicine.

The swift rise of "scientific" medicine over the past two centuries looks especially spectacular because it was starting from such an abysmal level. Throughout the Middle Ages, European medicine, like that in most societies then in Asia, Africa, and the Americas, was based mainly on empirical methodology, passed on orally from generation to generation. Because the large skull of human babies often necessitates assistance in the birth process, all peoples have had to learn basic principles of obstetrics. In Europe, as elsewhere, the people who provided obstetric care were of course almost all women. Because Europe was largely agricultural, other medical tasks fell largely to village healers, usually also women. These healers reset broken bones, performed operations including abortions, provided contraceptives, and diagnosed many diseases. They assembled a massive pharmacology of herbal remedies, many still in use, including digitalis (foxglove) to treat heart disease; ergot derivatives and belladonna to accelerate or inhibit uterine contractions; and a wide assortment of painkillers, digestive aids, and anti-inflammatory agents. Like most medical practitioners today, they also used incantations and rituals to promote the psychological component of their healing arts.

A Male-Dominated Profession

Because these healers were mainly women and because they excluded men from the birth scene, they posed a threat to male prerogatives. They also posed a threat to the church, which of course excluded them from the rival profession of priest, a man supposedly able to cure diseases through divine intervention. But their most direct threat was to the *profession* of medicine, reserved for a handful of men who studied at universities. The thirteenth century, when the Holy Roman Emperor Frederick II decreed that no one could practice medicine until he had been publicly approved by the masters of the University of Salerno, was also the century when the witch hunts began.

From the thirteenth through the seventeenth century, just as the all-male, university-trained medical profession was becoming hegemonic, women healers found themselves labeled as witches, tortured until they confessed that their powers came from Satan, and then hanged or burned alive. By the time the European witch hunts were over, the infrastructure of the traditional European health-care system had been shattered. In its place was a system that largely disdained empirical methods, basing itself on theory inherited from classical texts and using a variety of medical instruments derived from developing technology. What we call "scientific" medicine arose from the ruins of a female medicine that was probably more scientific than the early forms of its male successor.

By the eighteenth century, men were invading midwifery, the last preserve of female healing. (Men had a monopoly on obstetrical instruments, such as forceps, because women were legally barred from surgery.) The displacement of midwives by male physicians was deplored by Mary Wollstonecraft in her great 1792 manifesto, *A Vindication of the Rights of Woman.*

Common Sense Is Usurped

Five years later, Wollstonecraft chose a female midwife to attend her own delivery. The baby—the future author of *Frankenstein*—was delivered normally, but when the midwife was unable to extract the placenta, which had disintegrated, the chief obstetrician of a famous lying-in hospital was brought in. With unwashed hands, he groped for hours in her womb, almost certainly introducing puerperal fever, from which Wollstonecraft died ten days later. Not until 1843, when Dr. Oliver Wendell Holmes published *The Contagiousness of Puerperal Fever*, did Western medicine begin to comprehend why the mortality rate among women giving birth in European hospitals was between 20 and 30 percent. In 1847, [Hungarian physician] Ignaz Semmelweis noted that women who gave birth at home, tended by traditional midwives, had a far lower mortality rate and that in his own hospital women attended by physicians had a death rate from puerperal fever three times higher than the rate in the division where only midwives attended. When he had doctors wash their hands before obstetrical examinations and delivery, the death rate from puerperal fever immediately plunged from nearly 20 percent to 1.3 percent.

By the early nineteenth century, university-trained professional doctors—all male—had become the main deliverers of health care in Europe, England, and America for the upper and middle classes, especially in urban settings. Most doctors had been taught to rely on what were called heroic measures: massive bleeding, huge doses of laxatives and cathartics (including calomel, a salt of mercury), emetics, and, somewhat later, opium. Holmes expressed his contempt for the medicine being practiced by his professional contemporaries when he said that if all the medicines they used were thrown into the ocean, it would be better for people and worse for fish.

Mary Shelley's Experience with Birth and Death

One matrix for Mary Shelley's imagination was her own experience with birth and death in the medical environment of the early nineteenth century. Only one of her four children lived past the age of three. Her first child, born in 1815, died after twelve days. A few days later, seventeen-year-old Mary wrote in her journal: "Dream that my little baby came to life again; that it had only been cold, and that we had rubbed it before the fire, and it had lived."

Nine months after this journal entry, Mary gave birth to her son William, the namesake of Victor Frankenstein's young brother, the monster's first victim. Within months of William's birth, Mary began writing *Frankenstein*, which she completed in May 1817 while pregnant with her second daughter, Clara. *Frankenstein* was published in January 1818. Clara died that September, at the age of one. William died the following June, at the age of three, after a highly regarded physician prescribed massive doses of calomel, gamboge, and other purgatives for worms. This experience with European medicine evidently influenced revisions Mary Shelley made to the 1831 edition of *Frankenstein*, which she referred to in her introduction as "my hideous progeny."

Victor Frankenstein grows up with Elizabeth, a beautiful little girl whom he calls "my more than sister." In the 1831 edition, Elizabeth's mother, like Mary Shelley's, "had died on giving her birth," leading to her adoption by Victor's parents. Just as Victor is about to set off to begin his studies at the University of Ingolstadt, the first fatal event in his life occurs.

Elizabeth contracts scarlet fever and is "in the greatest danger." Victor's mother insists on attending "her sick bed,—her watchful attentions triumphed over the malignity of the distemper,—Elizabeth was saved, but the consequences of this imprudence were fatal to her preserver." His mother catches the disease and dies within three days as "her medical attendants" look on helplessly. On her deathbed, she joins the hands of Victor and Elizabeth and pledges them to marry each other. Elizabeth, thanks to the impotent medical care available, has now caused the death of both her birth mother and her adoptive mother.

Medicine and Male Hubris

It is prior to his mother's death and his study at Ingolstadt that Frankenstein, his imagination possessed by reading medieval alchemists, aspires to "banish disease from the human frame, and render man invulnerable to any but a violent death." But when he "becomes capable of bestowing animation upon lifeless matter," his goal shifts. He no longer seems concerned with either the prevention or the treatment of disease. What he now dedicates his life to is "the creation of a human being."

At this point, I raise the gender issues at the heart of Mary Shelley's prevision of modern science. I ask the class, If Frankenstein simply wants to create a human being, wouldn't there be an easier way to go about it? They point out that this would involve having sex with Elizabeth or some other woman. So what he wants to do is create a human being all by himself, without any contact with a woman, substituting for sexual and human intercourse what he construes to be science. To make his creature, he has already cut himself off entirely from all communication with Elizabeth, whom he claims to love so passionately. Later, when his father suggests that he marry Elizabeth, Victor recoils: "[T]o me the idea of an immediate union with my Elizabeth was one of horror and dismay." This is *before* the monster, a creature that has emerged from Frankenstein's mind and body, threatens, "I shall be with you on your wedding-night." On the wedding night, Victor has this to say to his bride: "Oh! peace, peace, my love [...] this night and all will be safe: but this night is dreadful, very dreadful." Then despite the obvious fact that the creature plans to kill Elizabeth, Victor sends her alone to their bridal bed while he, armed with sword and pistol, waits for the monster to attack *him*. The psychological significance of Victor's obsession had come out clearly in the dream he had the night he created his monster: "I thought I saw Elizabeth, in the bloom of health, walking in the streets of Ingolstadt. Delighted and surprised, I embraced her; but as I imprinted the first kiss on her lips, they became livid with the hue of death; her features appeared to change, and I thought that I held the corpse of my dead mother in my arms; a shroud enveloped her form, and I saw the graveworms crawling in the folds of the flannel." We do not need [Austrian psychologist Sigmund] Freud's *The Interpretation of Dreams*, published more than eight decades later, to recognize that Frankenstein's monster emerges from the unconscious depths of his masculine mind.

Disease, death, and the hubris of European medicine continued to haunt the imagination that conceived *Frankenstein*. Between the 1818 and 1831 editions, Mary Shelley brought forth one of the bleakest books in literature, *The Last Man* (1826), the first novel to imagine a disease that brings about the extinction of the human species. Entirely absent from *The Last Man* is Victor Frankenstein's boundless faith in scientific medicine.

Frankenstein Is a Mad Scientist Who Attempts to Revise Nature

Anne K. Mellor

Anne K. Mellor has served as professor of English at University of California, Los Angeles. She specializes in the Romantic era in Great Britain. Among her works are Mothers of the Nation: Women's Political Writing in England, 1780–1830; Mary Shelley: Her Life, Her Fiction, Her Monsters; *and* Romanticism and Gender.

Mary Shelley had no personal experience in the sciences, observes Mellor in the following selection, but she did have a sound grasp of the important scientific research being done during her lifetime. Frankenstein *is a powerful critique of scientific thought and of the role of the scientist in society, Mellor asserts. The novel explores the paradigm in which a male scientist attempts to force nature to abide by his will. In this regard, the author argues,* Frankenstein *is a feminist novel in which Victor Frankenstein's attempt to steal female control over biological reproduction leads to his destruction.*

*F*rankenstein offers a powerful critique both of scientific thought and of the psychology of the modern scientist. Mary Shelley may have been the first to question the commitment of science to the search for objective truth whatever the consequences. What science did Mary Shelley know? Clearly, she had no personal experience with scientific research: she envisioned Frankenstein's laboratory as a small attic room lit by a single candle! Nonetheless, she had a sound grasp of the concepts and implications of some of the most important scientific research of her day, namely the work of [British chemist and inventor] Sir Humphry Davy, [English physician] Erasmus Darwin and [Italian physician and physicist] Luigi Galvani.

Natural Philosophy's Mastery over Nature

Victor Frankenstein chooses to specialize at the University of Ingolstadt in the field of "natural philosophy" or chemical physiology, the field defined by Humphry Davy in his *A Discourse, Introductory to a Course of Lectures on Chemistry* (1802), the source for Professor Waldman's lecture in the novel. In this pamphlet, Davy insisted that modern chemistry has bestowed upon the chemist:

> ... powers which may be almost called creative; which have enabled him to modify and change the beings surrounding him, and by his experiments to interrogate nature with power, not simply as a scholar, passive and seeking only to understand her operations, but rather as a master, active with his own instruments.

Defining nature as female, Davy delineated two scientific ways of dealing with her. One could practice what we might call "descriptive" science, an effort to understand the workings of Mother Nature. Or one could practice an "interventionist" science, an effort to change the ways of nature. Davy clearly preferred the latter, hailing the scientist who modified nature as a "master." Similarly, Professor Waldman urges Victor Frankenstein to "penetrate into the recesses of nature, and show how she works in her hiding places," an effort Victor undertakes so that he might discover the "secret of life" and use it to his own ends. In Mary Shelley's view, such interventionist science is bad science, dangerous and self-serving.

In contrast, good science is that practised by Erasmus Darwin, the first theorist of evolution and grand uncle to Charles

Darwin [naturalist and author of *Origin of the Species*]. In *The Botanic Garden* (1791), [Erasmus] Darwin had described the evolution of more complex life forms from simpler ones, arguing that sexual propagation is higher on the evolutionary ladder than asexual propagation. From Darwin's perspective, Victor Frankenstein's experiment would reverse evolutionary progress, not only because Frankenstein reproduces asexually, but also because he constructs his new species from parts male and female, human and nonhuman. Moreover, he defies the entire concept of evolution by attempting to create a "new" species all at once, rather than by the random mutation of existing species.

Electricity as the Life Force

The scientist who had the most direct impact on Shelley's representation of Frankenstein's experiment was Luigi Galvani, who argued that the life force was electricity, and who had performed numerous experiments conducting electrical currents through dead animals in order to revive them. His most notorious experiment was performed in public in London on January 17, 1803, by his nephew Giovanni Aldini. On that day, Aldini applied galvanic electricity to the corpse of a human being. The body of the recently hanged criminal Thomas Forster was brought from Newgate Prison to Mr. Wilson's Anatomical Theatre, where live wires attached to a pile composed of 120 plates of zinc and 120 plates of copper were connected to the ear and mouth of the dead man. At this moment, Aldini reported, "the jaw began to quiver, the adjoining muscles were horribly contorted, and the left eye actually opened." When the wires were applied to the ear and rectum, they "excited in the muscles contractions much stronger ... The action even of those muscles furthest distant from the points of contact with the arc was so much increased as almost to give an appearance of re-animation.... The effect in this case surpassed our most sanguine expectations," Aldini said, concluding, "... vitality might, perhaps, have been restored, if many

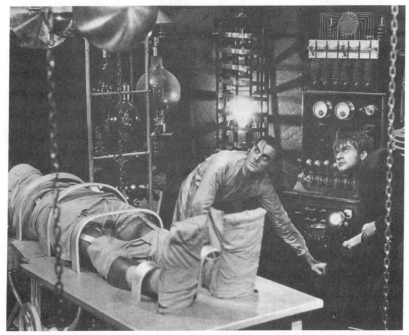

Dr. Henry Frankenstein (Colin Clive) and his assistant Fritz (Dwight Frye) attempt to re-store life to a human corpse in the 1931 film Frankenstein. *The character of Dr. Franken-stein typifies that of a "mad scientist."* © Bettmann/Corbis.

circumstances had not rendered it impossible." Here is the sci-entific prototype for Victor Frankenstein, restoring life to dead human corpses.

Victor as Mad Scientist

By grounding her literary vision of a scientist animating a corpse upon the cutting edge of science of her day, Mary Shelley initiated the new literary genre of science fiction. As Brian Aldiss and Robert Scholes have argued, *Frankenstein* possesses the three characteristics essential to the genre of sci-ence fiction: it is based on valid scientific research; it gives a persuasive prediction of what science might achieve in the fu-ture; and it offers a humanistic critique of the benefits and dangers of either a specific scientific milestone or of the na-ture of scientific thought.

Frankenstein is notable both for its grasp of the nature of the scientific enterprise and for its searching analysis of the dangers inherent in that enterprise. Victor Frankenstein is our first literary portrait of what we might now call the "mad scientist," but a far more subtle one than that provided by such films as Stanley Kubrick's *Dr. Strangelove*. Mary Shelley recognized that Victor Frankenstein's passion for scientific research is a displacement of normal emotions and healthy affections. Significantly, when Victor is working on his experiment, he cannot love: he ignores his family, even his fiancée Elizabeth, and takes no pleasure in the beauties of nature. Moreover, he becomes physically and mentally ill, subject to nervous fevers.

Shelley's Critique of Scientific Thought

Mary Shelley also offers a critique of the very nature of scientific thought. Inherent in the concept of science is a potent gender dichotomy, as Sir Humphry Davy assumed: nature is female, the scientist is male. The scientist who analyses, manipulates and attempts to control nature is engaging in a politics that today we would call sexism. [English philosopher and statesman] Francis Bacon heralded the seventeenth-century scientific revolution: "I am come in very truth leading to you Nature with all her children to bind her to your service and make her your slave." By constructing nature as female, the scientist feels entitled to exploit her to gratify his own desire for power, money, status. Frankenstein's scientific quest is nothing less than an attempt to "penetrate into the recesses of nature, and show how she works in her hiding places," to penetrate her womb and to appropriate it, to steal female biological reproduction. In effect, Frankenstein wishes to rape nature in order to gratify his own lust for power. As Frankenstein fantasizes, "A new species would bless me as its creator and source; many happy and excellent natures would owe their being to me. No father could claim the gratitude of his child so completely as I should deserve theirs." If Frankenstein were to succeed in stealing the power of female biological reproduction, he would eliminate the biological necessity for females as such; the human race of males could survive by cloning. This is why he rips up the half-constructed female creature: he wishes to destroy the ability of an independent female to create a new race of her own. Frankenstein's hostility to female sexuality as such is perhaps the greatest horror, for women readers, of Mary Shelley's story: Frankenstein poses a threat to the very social and biological survival of the human female.

Feminism and the Male Scientist

In Mary Shelley's feminist novel, however, Victor Frankenstein does not succeed in creating a new race of supermen who can survive without women. Mother Nature fights back. She begins by plaguing Frankenstein with bad health: as he engages in his two experiments, he is tormented by fevers, heart palpitations, nervous fits, depression and paranoia. His physical exhaustion is finally so great that he dies at the age of twenty-five. Nature further punishes Victor, thwarting his creation of a normal child: his lack of empathy and maternal bonding first causes him to create a giant—the "minuteness of the [normal-sized] parts formed a great hindrance to my speed"— and then prevents him from normal procreation with his bride Elizabeth, whom he abandons to his creature on their wedding night. Finally, nature pursues Victor Frankenstein with the very electricity and fire he has stolen from her. The lightning, thunder and rain that flashes around Victor as he carries on his experiments are not just the conventional atmospheric effects of the Gothic novel, but also a manifestation of nature's elemental powers. Like the classical Greek Furies, nature pursues Victor to his hiding places, destroying not only Victor but his family, friend, and servant. Finally, the penalty of violating nature is death.

Mary Shelley's novel offers an alternative to Victor's and [character Robert] Walton's view of nature as a female to be penetrated and possessed by the male scientist, or as merely dead matter to be reassembled at his will. Significantly, the only member of the Frankenstein family still alive at the end of the novel is Ernest, who wished to become a farmer, not a manipulative and oppressive lawyer like his father. His survival, together with [Victor's friend Henry] Clerval's enthusiastic love of the changing beauty of nature's seasons, reveals Mary Shelley's own view of the appropriate relationship between human beings and nature: a vision of nature as a person with rights and responsibilities who must be treated with respect, even reverence. Only if we can learn to embrace even nature's freaks and monsters with the understanding love of a mother can we avoid the fate of Frankenstein. As the creature reminds Victor, "You are my creator but I am your master—obey!"

Frankenstein Taps into Biotechnical Desires and Fears

Jon Turney

Jon Turney has served as science editor of the Times Higher Education Supplement *and as a senior lecturer in science communication in the Department of Science and Technology Studies at University College, London.*

In the following selection Turney explores why the myth of Frankenstein has been so pervasive in Western culture since Mary Shelley wrote her novel. Despite the novel's limited interest in actual science, and the mere thirty pages of the novel that Shelley devotes to the creation of the monster, it is the novel's scientific themes that continue to attract readers and viewers of the numerous cinematic versions of the novel. Biotechnology, the science that forms the basis of Shelley's novel, is no ordinary science, according to Turney. People are always more interested in it than in other sciences. During the Industrial Revolution nature and the human body were always viewed as separate and opposed to technology and machines. But Shelley connects the two, conceiving of a story where technology transforms the human body directly. This scientific power over the body, Turney asserts, is both desired and dreaded—and the dichotomy lends great influence to the Frankenstein mythology.

The accumulated retellings of the *Frankenstein* myth are now so numerous as almost to defy empirical analysis. Today, we encounter Frankenstein in many forms. Any of the old films may still be seen as late-night TV fillers, or on video. There are even two films which incorporate versions of the origin myth of the novel, mixing together the story of Mary

[Shelley], Percy [Bysshe Shelley, Mary's husband] and [poet Lord] Byron by the lakeside [Lake Geneva] with the creation of the monster. New films continue to incorporate elements of the story, from *Demon Seed*, in which the monster is a computer which finds a way of inseminating a human female, to *Robocop*. Numerous editions of the novel remain in print, and new variations on the story continue to appear in printed fiction. Some of these, like [English writer] Steven Gallagher's *Chimera*, are filmed in turn. Others, like [English writer] Hilary Bailey's striking *Frankenstein's Bride*, remain as solely literary efforts. . . . [It] is clear that the form of the story still appeals to artists in several media.

In addition, as with all truly frightening myths, we have tried to tame *Frankenstein* by making fun of it. [Actor Boris] Karloff's monster [from the 1931 film] has been domesticated, in media ranging from the 1960s US television series *The Munsters* to the British children's comic the *Beano*, which features Frankie Stein. A distant descendant of Karloff even featured as Frank in the British Conservative government's television commercials for shares in its soon to be privatised electricity generation concern in the early 1990s. This taken-for-grantedness shows how well the cultural script has been learned. In consequence, the single word 'Frankenstein' is seen constantly as a metaphor in media commentary of all kinds, especially political commentary.

Pervasiveness of the Frankenstein Myth

Why, then, has the story endured? Is it simply because the frame is so open at various points that it is infinitely adaptable? Or are there particular reasons, culturally general enough to read across all the retellings, with all their differences of detail, yet still specific to the culture which we share with Mary Shelley—broadly, the culture of modernity?

The first answer is to try to isolate what has endured in all the renderings of the myth since 1818. The story, for all its familiarity, is still a frightening one. It is frightening because it depicts a human enterprise which is out of control, and which turns on its creator. So much carries over from the earlier myths about the getting of knowledge. But *Frankenstein* is about science. What is more, the science is pursued, if not always with the best of intentions, then for motives with which we can readily identify. In the most striking retellings, the myth is never a straightforward anti-science story. There is something admirable about Victor Frankenstein, about Henry Frankenstein in [American director] James Whale's film, even about [English actor] Peter Cushing's Baron Frankenstein. Even so, our sympathies are always torn between Frankenstein and his monster. The *Frankenstein* script, in its most salient forms, incorporates an ambivalence about science, method and motive, which is never resolved.

The retention of science in all the later derivatives of the story is the most striking feature of the myth. After all, in the original text, once Victor's narrative begins, the creation of the monster is accomplished in a scant thirty pages, in which space is also given to the background and education of the monster's creator. The scientific details are few. After Victor's 'brilliant light' dawns we never learn more than how he eventually 'collected the instruments of life around me, that I might infuse a spark of life into the lifeless thing that lay at my feet'. Yet it is those first thirty pages that supply the seeds of almost all of the images derived from *Frankenstein* which appear in so many variations in later stories about science and scientists.

Science Entices the Scientist

Among others, we can distinguish in *Frankenstein* models for the scientist whose good intentions blind him to the true nature of his enterprise: 'wealth was an inferior object; but what glory would attend the discovery if I could banish disease from the human frame and render man invulnerable to any but a violent death!' Victor proclaims. And so say all of us mortal readers. But Victor also personifies the scientist as Faustian knowledge-seeker [referring to a character who sold his soul to the devil]; 'the world was to me a secret which I desired to divine', he remembers, and he recalls that 'none but those who have experienced them can conceive of the enticements of science' or, as a narrow materialist, 'On my education my father had taken the greatest precautions that my mind should be impressed with no supernatural horrors ... a churchyard was to me merely the receptacle of bodies deprived of life.' There are also hints that science has some drive of its own, external to the will of the scientist and eventually overwhelming him. 'Natural philosophy', Victor reflects sadly, 'is the genius that has regulated my fate.' Amidst all the simplifications, deletions and elaborations of the original, the identification of Victor as a scientist has remained inviolate. It is science which gives him his success, and that success gives him power over life. Even though his character was first drawn before biology was a separate discipline, Frankenstein is always a proto-biologist.

So the endurance of the myth plainly does testify to a deep disquiet at the potentialities inherent in scientific discovery in general, and the science of life in particular. And it is a disquiet which Mary Shelley appears to have tapped into at a remarkably early stage in the development of modern life science. The appearance of the story, and its ready acceptance, so soon after [English physician] Erasmus Darwin's speculations were published, suggest that unease at the prospect of science attaining powers over life is readily evoked in the public mind. So I agree with all those who have suggested that the *Frankenstein* myth both expresses and reinforces an undercurrent of feelings about science; that in [Professor and literary critic] George Levine's phrase, it 'articulates a deeply felt cultural neurosis'. But what, exactly, does this neurosis consist of?

No Ordinary Science

It is clear that what we now call biomedical science, or the possibility of a technologically effective biology, has played a key role in shaping the modern attitude to science. We have always been prisoners of the body, victims of morbidity and mortality, and we desire the power that biology might give us to relieve these burdens. In more recent times, this can be seen from other kinds of evidence. Medical and biological stories have long accounted for a large proportion of the press reporting of science, for example. Editors appear to regard such stories as of more interest to their readers than other scientific items. The news-consuming public, in consequence, may be more aware of events in biological science than in other fields. The nature of their interest has also been long established. Turn the pages of a major newspaper from the early years of this century [twentieth], the *San Francisco Chronicle,* say, and you will find front-page stories on radical new surgical procedures, on the possibility of choosing the sex of a baby, on proposed scientific techniques for prolonging life, and on putative cures for cancer. These stories show the early convergence of news values and the territory of biomedicine. Biological research and medical practice mean birth, sex and death; suffering, disease and disability.

Biologists who become visible to the public are aware of the hopes and fears their science raises. As the French geneticist and popular writer Jean Rostand . . . attested in the 1950s: 'The best way to gain an idea of what the human, *emotional* value of biology can be, is to look through some of the strange correspondence that a biologist receives . . . people take him for a magician, a healer, a confessor, a friend.'

Biotechnical Advances Are Always in Demand

Among the letters he describes are those from couples seeking to replace a lost child with a perfect twin, queries on the consequences of mixed marriage, people seeking confirmation of paternity by blood typing, enhancement of their children's intelligence, rejuvenation for the elderly, sex changes or cures for infertility. Rostand concludes that 'the science that provokes such appeals, prayers and confessions, the science that penetrates into private life, and whose warnings or advice can influence a marriage, a decision to have children, a person's destiny, is no ordinary science'.

These examples express very well the idea that biology is indeed 'no ordinary science' for the public. It is the science which touches on the most potent wishes of human life. The realisation that biology offers the prospect of ultimate control over or transformation of the living realm, just as physical science controls and transforms the physical environment, thus evokes deep-rooted feelings. This realisation by itself can produce either positive or negative reactions, and *a priori* [necessarily] both may seem equally likely. Indeed, . . . the first great practical successes of scientific medicine produced more general endorsement of the virtues of science than ever before. Yet, the response to a genuinely effective experimental biology has always had its negative side as well. To understand *Frankenstein*, we need to look further into the roots of that ambivalence.

One set of clues here comes from early responses to industrialisation, and to the conspicuously powerful applications of physico-chemical technology which it highlighted. These responses were bound up in complex ways with changing awareness of the natural world, and particularly of the body. A number of writers have suggested that the body is the locus for a set of feelings which play a major part in determining responses to the effects of industrialisation.

The Body Versus the Machine

The transforming potential of physico-chemical technology was made manifest in the most concrete way in the eighteenth and nineteenth centuries, and the evidence was beginning to be apparent to all when *Frankenstein* was written. The impact of technology differentiated the industrial revolution from the past in ways that were hard not to notice, as the machine transformed entire landscapes. The ensuing cultural changes, which expressed or embodied responses to the vastly expanded role of technology while these changes were actually taking place and first being recognised as being revolutionary in scope, are complex and hard to summarise. . . .

There is a contradiction between our spontaneous, visceral experience of the world, mediated through the senses, and our technological capacity to order the world through analysis and measurement. Faced with this contradiction, one possible response to the objectification of the world by science and technology is a 'recoil to the body', a reaffirmation of the intensity of bodily feelings and of the integrity of the person. Thus the body, as an image of the natural world in microcosm, becomes a metaphoric resource for those who criticise the scientific world-view.

Studies of the responses to the machine—as a symbol of modern technology—in Victorian literature, find that there is a consistent pattern of opposition between the mechanistic and the organic. Mechanism and machines are employed to represent the scientific mind, while the organic represents a set of qualities associated with the living organism. Mechanism implies fixed causality, determinism, lawfulness, all of which are opposed to the irregularity, wholeness and intuitive harmony supposedly found in the natural world. In all of these studies, images of the natural world are an inspiration for opposition to the scientific world-view and to the effects of the objects and artefacts deriving from that science.

But a science of life put this strategy in question. . . . If those who viewed physical science with distaste [the vitalists] sought to retreat to the comforting haven of the living world, science [in effect, the mechanists] sought to mechanise even that. Here is one reason for the bitterness of the recurrent disputes between mechanists and vitalists, and also for the belief that perceptions of the likely development of biology may have played an especially large part in sustaining ambivalence about science. The growing abstraction of biological work can become a symbol, for some, of the estrangement of man from nature brought about by industrialisation.

The Faustian Myth

There is a yet wider dimension to this history, and to biology's potential significance. Taking its measure involves a broader account of the changes which were in train during Mary Shelley's early life, changes which are not completely captured by speaking of the industrial revolution. They are the changes, of which startling technological progress was only one element, that marked the beginning of modernity. We can see how the creative imagination could intuit the ultimate implications of these wider changes by looking at a reading of another myth, one closely related to *Frankenstein*. The reading I want to examine is [American philosopher] Marshall Berman's study of [Johann Wolfgang von Goethe's tragic play] *Faust* as a myth of modernity. . . .

Berman's view of the experience of modernity [is] one of forces unleashed, of unlimited change in all spheres of life. . . .

Berman tells us, the most penetrating analysis of the course of modernity came from Goethe, and can be found in his extended version of the Faust myth. Goethe's *Faust*, begun in 1770 and finished sixty years later, when Goethe was 82, is the work of a writer of far greater powers than Mary Shelley, and is justly celebrated as one of the great works of European literature. For Berman, the work, and especially *Faust Part Two*, is a reflection on Goethe's own experience of the second phase of modernity: 'the work was in process all through one of the most turbulent and revolutionary eras in the history of the world . . . the whole movement of the work enacts the larger movement of Western society'.

In Part Two, which Berman calls the tragedy of development, Faust uses the power granted him by Mephistopheles [the devil] to transform a whole landscape. He is no longer satisfied with the good things sought by earlier Fausts. Money, sex, power and glory are not enough. He wants to refashion the world, and creates the technological and social organisation to do it. The whole of Part Two, according to Berman, is a parable about modern progress, and 'Goethe's point is that the deepest horrors of Faustian development spring from its most honorable aims and its most authentic achievements'.

Shelley Proposes the Direct Transformation of the Body

Now there is much to be said for Berman's reading of *Faust*, and it is certainly true that the story is still one of our most powerful myths. But, when we compare it to *Frankenstein*, it is evident that Goethe's modern myth is only a partial transformation of the older stories of Faust. Mary Shelley, writing in the same period, and confronting many of the same concerns, created a story which is more deserving of the title of a modern myth. While Faust, for all his recognisably modern outlook, still relies on a pact with the devil to secure his power, and pays the price, Frankenstein achieves his powers unaided. The Englishwoman's story is a modern myth because it is grounded in science, not the supernatural.

That, though, is not the only significant respect in which she differs from Goethe, in spite of all they share in terms of intellectual influence and sensibility. Faust is preoccupied with operating on the world, with physical and social transformation. Man will be transformed in the new world, but only through all the other changes Faust brings about. Frankenstein, on the other hand, is set on transforming humans directly. If he can discover the secret of life, then he can father a new species. To do so, he will experiment directly on the body.

Here, I think, Mary intuited the power of a threat which would come to seem graver as time went by. In a world where everything appeared to be subject to change . . . there was one sphere of existence which was exempt. The natural world, although it could be reshaped by physical onslaught on the landscape, although it could be despoiled or laid waste, was not yet open to technological manipulation. The forms and varieties of creatures, the hierarchy of species, the biological imperatives of existence, were fixed points in an ever-changing world.

Power over the Body

The human body, too, as I have suggested, provided an unchanging ground for experience of other changes. This does not mean, of course, that *experience* of the body, or ideas about its constitution, did not change. But the body itself was not seen as changing by those experiencing the first rush of modernity. While the dead body had been anatomised for two centuries, in pursuit of a science of the interior which had made a deep impression on Renaissance and early modern culture, that science was still largely descriptive. The living body was not yet susceptible to the kind of science being developed in other areas, in which 'the object to be known . . . will be known in such a way that it can be changed'. Frankenstein the character, and *Frankenstein* the novel, are both steeped in the anatomical tradition. But this anatomist goes further. Mary Shelley made the necessary imaginative leap, and fashioned an image of a science working on the body to transform it, a science which might one day come to pass. Now that we are indeed building such a science, we can see that it has always been a part of the modern project. She saw this right at the start. If, as Berman says, Goethe's key insight is the ambivalence stemming from the fact that 'the deepest horrors of Faustian development spring from its most honorable aims and its most authentic achievements', then the best horror story would be rooted in the power which we simultaneously most desire, and most dread: power over the body. *Frankenstein* focused attention on that prospect nearly two centuries ago. We still feel the pull of the story because that power is now ours for the asking.

Artificial Creatures of Modern Films Renew Sympathy for Frankenstein's Creation

Jay Clayton

Jay Clayton has served as Professor of English at Vanderbilt University. He is the author of Romantic Vision and the Novel, The Pleasures of Babel: Contemporary Literature and Theory, *and* Charles Dickens in Cyberspace.

According to Clayton in the following selection, of all the descendents of Mary Shelley's monster, most are evil creatures whose creators have sent them out as object lessons about the risks of unchecked scientific pursuit. Only recently have authors and film directors created benign robots and other artificially intelligent creatures. But, Clayton argues, Shelley's original novel, published in 1818, was not so much critiquing hazardous scientific pursuit as it was pointing out the danger of Romantic egotism, as personified by Victor Frankenstein. It was only in the 1831 edition, Clayton explains, that Shelley intensified her criticism of the mad scientist.

> If the power of reflecting on the past, and darting the keen eye of contemplation into futurity, be the grand privilege of man, it must be granted that some people enjoy this prerogative in a very limited degree. Every thing new appears to them wrong; and not able to distinguish the possible from the monstrous, they fear where no fear should find a place, running from the light of reason, as if it were a firebrand.

> —*Mary Wollstonecraft [Mary Shelley's mother]*,
> A Vindication of the Rights of Woman *(1792)*

In an age of reproductive technology, cloning, artificial intelligence, and robotics, has *Frankenstein*'s futurity come to pass? Are we living in the time Mary Shelley foreshadowed? Perhaps so, although the author did not think of her work as prophesying the future. Shelley was much more interested in the science of her own day than in looking ahead. She uses the word "futurity," an old-fashioned noun meaning a time to come, only once in the novel, and it has nothing to do with fearful prophecies. Rather, it appears in a letter Elizabeth Lavenza writes to reassure Victor that she still wants to marry him; he plays a lead role, she tells him, in all her "airy dreams of futurity." Though Mary Shelley, writing in 1816, set her novel in the late eighteenth century, *Frankenstein*, perhaps more than any other novel, has been interpreted as a warning about impending events. As a cautionary tale, *Frankenstein* has had an illustrious career; virtually every catastrophe of the last two centuries—revolution, rampant industrialism, epidemics, famines, World War I, Nazism, nuclear holocaust, clones, replicants, and robots—has been symbolized by Shelley's monster. If Shelley's work is the first futuristic novel, as some critics have claimed, then the genre of science fiction was inaugurated as a warning, not a promise, about the world of tomorrow.

The Positive Side of Artificial Life

In recent years, however, something has changed. Against all odds, a few influential writers and artists have begun to interpret Shelley's tale of a modern Prometheus [a titan of Greek mythology whose name means forethought] as promising things they would like to see happen in real life. These people make up an eclectic collection, including Hollywood filmmakers such as Ridley Scott, George Lucas, and Steven Spielberg; science fiction writers Nancy Kress and Octavia A. Butler; pioneers of robotics Hans Moravec and Rodney A. Brooks; the visionary inventor Ray Kurzweil; the feminist theorist of science studies Donna Haraway; the hypertext author Shelley Jackson, and others. Each of these figures uses the legacy of *Frankenstein*, either implicitly or explicitly, to register some positive views of a future containing artificial creatures. . . . These new conceptions [can be traced in] the way they transform Shelley's vision through several key works—Ridley Scott's *Blade Runner* (1982), Shelley Jackson's *Patchwork Girl* (1995), Hans Moravec's *Robot* (1999), Steven Spielberg's *A.I.: Artificial Intelligence* (2001), and Rodney Brooks's *Flesh and Machines* (2002). Sympathetic descendants of Frankenstein's Creature remain a tiny minority, almost lost among the multitude of demons stalking popular culture, but their emergence today is worth analyzing.

This development takes two forms: first, revisions that explore genetic and reproductive technology; second, those that reimagine *Frankenstein* in a world of cyborgs, artificial intelligence (AI), artificial life (AL), and robotics. In terms of genetics, the influence of *Blade Runner* has been unparalleled. The "replicants" in this movie are entirely biological creatures, designed by genetic engineers in the early twenty-first century to be "off-world" slaves on space colonies. When four stage a violent escape and return to earth to find their maker, they are hunted down and killed as dangerous monsters. The movie powerfully evokes *Frankenstein*, but concludes by converting its hero to the replicants' cause. The artificial creatures end up seeming more "human" than the people who stalk them.

The second line of descendants from *Frankenstein* are characterized by mechanical components and computer intelligence. Though the Creature in Shelley's novel was made up entirely of flesh and blood, filmmakers, and, later, science fiction novelists, have added a mechanical dimension of increasing complexity to her creation. Most of these later creatures continued to be viewed as monstrous, in keeping with their horror genre roots, but a different attitude began to take shape in the 1940s when [science fiction writer] Isaac Asimov's long-running and popular robot series [*I, Robot*] gave a positive spin to the idea of intelligent machines. Since then, scientists in the fields of AI and robotics have striven mightily to alter *Frankenstein's* legacy by crossing it with that of Asimov. Spielberg too invokes Asimov's *I, Robot* in interviews about *A.I.*, and the screenplay of another recent film, *Bicentennial Man* (1999), is adapted from an Asimov story [of the same name]. If asked, these recent exponents of artificial life would no doubt repudiate Shelley's cautionary vision, but they are her heirs nonetheless. As I shall show, affirmative visions of artificial life, no less than dire warnings against scientific hubris, possess strong ties to *Frankenstein*.

From Fear to Sympathy

It is easy to see how the novel serves the cause of those concerned that science has overstepped its bounds. In the biological arena, critics routinely label genetically modified agriculture "Frankenfood" and conjure up the specter of Shelley's monster to fight against reproductive cloning. In response to robotics, the monster still turns up in debates about automated machinery displacing workers (just as it did in nineteenth-century Luddite protests), and hostile computers in movies, from *2001: A Space Odyssey* to the *Terminator* series and *The Matrix*, mine the Frankenstein complex for some prophetic touches.

Demonstrating how affirmative perspectives on artificial life emerge from Shelley's text requires more detailed attention to the original work. Today's positive interpretations draw on an undercurrent in *Frankenstein*, to which feminist critics of the 1970s and 1980s first drew attention: the novel's sympathy for the Creature. Contemporary advocates of AI emphasize many of the same things Shelley did: the emotional vulnerability of this new being, its abandonment in a hostile world, existentially alone, its sheer *creatureliness*. Turning its artificial origins from a liability to a virtue, writers and filmmakers fo-

Frontispiece to the revised edition of Frankenstein *by Mary Shelley, published by Colburn and Bentley, London 1831.*

cus on what humans owe to the things they create. For example, a scientist in Spielberg's *A.I.* remarks, "If a robot could genuinely love a person, what responsibility does that person hold toward that Mecha in return?" Ridley Scott in *Blade Run-*

ner follows Shelley in associating the replicants both with Adam, fallen and in exile from his proper home, and with a Romantic version of Satan, noble in his defiance of the creator who has deserted him. Further, all of the filmmakers and writers considered here follow Shelley in using images of slavery, abandoned children, spurned love, and bitter loneliness to arouse fellow feeling in the public at large.

Shelley and "Good" Science

The most interesting parallel, however, exists because of a little-appreciated aspect of Shelley's text: its complex attitude toward the science of her own day. Shelley was hardly an unthinking opponent of what was then called "natural philosophy." As [literary critic] Anne K. Mellor has shown . . . Shelley distinguishes between "good" and "bad" science, the former epitomized by what she saw as [eighteenth-century physician] Erasmus Darwin's respect for nature, the latter by [eighteenth- and nineteenth-century scientists and inventors] Humphry Davy, Luigi Galvani, and Adam Walker's interventionist approaches. Like her mother, Mary Wollstonecraft, Shelley viewed favorably many forms of natural science, and she shared her mother's Enlightenment belief in intellectual progress, the virtue of education, and the rationality of women. The epigraph for this chapter captures something of Wollstonecraft's faith in futurity and her hope that the light of reason might disentangle the worthwhile from the monstrous in new ideas.

Similar positive views toward progress, including technological progress, are visible in *Frankenstein*, particularly in the first edition of 1818, alongside the indictments of scientific overreaching. Shelley's portrait of the ideal "man of science"—Frankenstein's admired professor Waldman—is sympathetically drawn: it combines an aversion to pedantry, dogmatism, and "petty experimentalis[m]" with frankness, good nature, and a commitment to a well-rounded, liberal approach to learning. In two passages that were cut from the 1831 version of the novel (that which most readers encountered, until the 1970s), Victor's father teaches him the properties of electricity by imitating Benjamin Franklin's experiment with a kite, and Victor himself works hard to acquire the main scholarly languages of the age and to master practical scientific advances such as distillation, the steam engine, and the air pump.

Scientific Hubris

Still, despite these favorable assessments of science, most readers come away from the book with an overwhelming impression of the dangers of scientific hubris. What makes matters confusing is that even the Enlightenment attitudes found in the 1818 version contain critiques of scientific inquiry. The rhetoric, however, is often different from the 1831 text. Notice the balanced cadence of an eighteenth-century moralist in this warning Frankenstein gives to Walton in the 1818 text: "Learn from me, if not by my precepts, at least by my example, how dangerous is the acquirement of knowledge, and how much happier that man is who believes his native town to be the world, than he who aspires to become greater than his nature will allow." Now compare it with this typical addition to the 1831 edition that dramatizes scientific overreaching: "So much has been done, exclaimed the soul of Frankenstein—more, far more, will I achieve: treading in the steps already marked, I will pioneer a new way, explore unknown powers, and unfold to the world the deepest mysteries of creation." In these additions, one finds all the Romantic motifs of madness and guilt, impenetrable mysteries, the tumult of the swelling heart, clearly marked as evidence of Frankenstein's terrible error.

A careful reader can trace both Enlightenment and Romantic versions of the author's indictments of her scientist hero. Frankenstein's scientific "enthusiasm" is condemned as self-centered and isolating in the 1818 version. The dangers of enthusiasm is a common Enlightenment theme, found throughout the works of [English writer] Samuel Johnson or [English novelist] Jane Austen, to pick two writers who have rarely been identified with Shelley. In the 1831 text, Shelley adds the language of madness, obsessive questing, and uncontrollable ambition. Here, in one such insertion, is Frankenstein warning Walton about scientific aspiration: "a groan burst from his heaving breast . . . at length he spoke, in broken accents—'Unhappy man! Do you share my madness? Have you drunk also of the intoxicating draught? Hear me—let me reveal my tale, and you will dash the cup from your lips!'" The final text stresses Frankenstein's "fervent longing to penetrate the secrets of nature," to rend the veil of this world with a violence that is identified as willful and characteristically masculine.

By eliminating many positive comments about science and by exaggerating Frankenstein's Romantic spirit, the 1831 text makes it difficult to distinguish between Shelley's measured critique of nineteenth-century science and her more flamboyant denunciations of the Romantic male ego. Although related, these two dimensions of the book can be distinguished. Shelley's target was never a thoughtful natural philosophy, especially when it was balanced by other branches of learning. When Shelley takes aim at Frankenstein's research, she criticizes the excesses of an overwrought sensibility, not natural philosophy itself. The craving for immortality, the hubris of trying to rival God, a foolish regard for alchemy, or a desire to usurp women's power of creation—these passions afflict other possessed souls in nineteenth-century literature, from [Goethe's] Faust and [Lord Byron's] Cain to [Herman] Melville's Ahab, and are hardly confined to mad scientists. Shelley's purpose in intensifying her rhetoric in the 1831 version is not to amplify the critique of science but to lay bare the dangers of Romantic egotism.

Frankenstein Points Out the Dilemma of All Science-Based Technology

Edward Tenner

Edward Tenner has taught at Rutgers University and Princeton University and served as a science editor at the Princeton University Press. He is the author of Our Own Devices: The Past and Future of Body Technology.

In this viewpoint Tenner discusses how, since the earliest days of technology, artists have charted the territory of rebellious machinery. As technology became more complex, and humans moved from using simple tools to managing complex systems, Tenner asserts that controlling such systems became more problematical. Mary Shelley poses the question, how can we understand a system before we attempt to change it? As a complex system, Victor Frankenstein's monster develops a will of its own and rebels against its creator. In Tenner's view such is the paradigm for all complex systems that may malfunction in unforeseen ways.

From the earliest days of the industrial age, the greatest artists and writers of the West have had their eyes on the recalcitrant and even malevolent machine. Human ingenuity mining against itself was not a new conceit. The perils of magic were well known. The medieval Jewish legend of the Golem had already inspired the story of a clay monster that was fashioned by Rabbi Löw of sixteenth-century Prague, only to turn against its creator. When Hamlet [in Shakespeare's play of the same title] declares it "sport to have the enginer /

Edward Tenner, *Why Things Bite Back: Technology and the Revenge of Unintended Consequences.* New York: Alfred A. Knopf, 1996. Copyright © 1996 by Edward Tenner. Reproduced by permission of Alfred A. Knopf, a division of Random House, Inc. In the UK by permission of Fourth Estate, a division of HarperCollins Publishers Ltd.

Hoist with his own petar," his metaphor was of a crude small bomb used to blow away a gate or part of a wall, sometimes taking its creator with it.

If men and women before 1800 or so had any idea of a malevolent machine, nobody knows about it. No student of early European popular culture I have asked has found an example of it. The elites who did most of the writing had little contact with the mechanics of a household. [Eighteenth-century Scottish economist] Adam Smith, in his *Theory of Moral Sentiments*, treats early mechanical consumer goods as playthings. The men who worked with the most complex and perilous machines of medieval and early modern Europe, sailors and miners, do not seem to have endowed ships and equipment with the malicious independent will so familiar to twentieth-century people. There were spirits *in* the mines—in America, the Tommy Knockers and the Old Man—who demanded respectful treatment and could help and rescue as well as bedevil. But these creatures were almost literally ghosts in the machine, not features of the shafts, pumps, or tools. Breaking a shipboard custom could threaten the safety of the vessel and crew, but not because the ship's design itself had hidden dangerous and refractory powers.

Nature's Revenge

In traditional lore, when nature took its revenge it was to punish sin. After the newly rich miners of a Polish town began to wear silver buckles on their shoes and throw bread in the street to protect them from the dirt, their mine was flooded and they had to go without bread. Pride, arrogance, exploitation, and avarice, not technological overreaching, brought disaster. These stories were entirely consistent with the early modern idea that nature itself would expose and defeat evil conduct.

Even a scientific figure as important as the eighteenth-century botanist [Carl] Linnaeus collected dozens of anecdotes to this effect in a secret notebook for his son [also named Carl], published only after the Second World War as *Nemesis Divina* [*Divine Justice*]. Linnaeus saw no opposition between the natural and the divine order. The powers of nature itself punished wrongdoers who had kept their secrets from their fellow men and women. Like calamities of the miners' lore, each of the natural disasters in Linnaeus avenged some moral transgression. And like the miners' stories, Linnaeus's parables—which read today like a mixture of [philosopher Søren] Kierkegaard and the *National Enquirer*—were not for a broad reading public but for a small, intimate circle.

The Real Frankenstein

It was Mary Shelley's *Frankenstein* that first connected Promethean [after the Titan in Greek mythology who betrays the gods to save humankind] technology with unintended havoc. The theme riveted audiences over a century before the most rudimentary organ transplantation was medically possible. The literary historian Steven Early Forry has shown how rapidly Shelley's story spread across the stages of London and Paris within a few years of its publication in 1818. In fact, the stock figures of mad scientist, cretinous assistant, and brutal monster probably owe more to these early stage versions than to Shelley's original text.

The Victor Frankenstein of the novel was no doctor—of either medicine or philosophy. But his project was a scientific and technological experiment, and he had left his studies at the University of Ingolstadt after a successful career in which he "had made some discoveries in the improvement of chemical instruments, which procured me great esteem and admiration in the university." He was a genteel amateur in the eighteenth-century mode, created just before the rise of nineteenth-century academic and industrial science.

Mary Shelley based her story on actual "galvanic" experiments wherein corpses were animated electrically. Was she warning against the conquest of nature by science, against male appropriation of life-giving power? A growing number of critics think so, perhaps reading certain twentieth-century attitudes into Shelley's story. Victor Frankenstein was reassembling and reviving life, not growing it. They are certainly right, though, in seeing in the book a revenge of nature against practitioners of a technology that surpasses their understanding.

Frankenstein's fateful error was to consider everything but the sum of the parts he had assembled. The "limbs were in proportion, and I had selected his features as beautiful." The hair was "of a lustrous black, and flowing; his teeth of a pearly whiteness." But he had failed to understand the body as a *system*. Thus the "yellow skin scarcely covered the work of muscles and arteries beneath," and the "watery eyes . . . seemed almost of the same color as the dun white sockets in which they were set."

Mary Shelley was pointing to a dilemma of all science-based technology—at a time when science was only starting to influence technological practice. How can we understand a system before we try to change it? Disaster inspires so much of our understanding. Victor Frankenstein had pursued years of steady research and development, punctuated by readings of the latest journals. "I prepared myself for a multitude of reverses; my operations might be incessantly baffled, and at last my work might be imperfect; yet, when I considered the improvement which every day takes place in science and mathematics, I was encouraged to hope my present attempts would at least lay the foundations of future success." And in fact Frankenstein's last words, after an unconvincing plea against the life of science, are: "Yet why do I say this? I have myself been blasted in these hopes, yet others may succeed."

From Tool to System: Transforming Revenge

Mary Shelley wrote prophetically at the dawn of technological systems thinking. She does not treat the monster as a machine, but neither is it human despite its articulate and moving speech. Still less is it an animal. Neither its creator nor any other person in the story gives it a name of its own. It is a kind of system, though, a creature with unintended emotions, including rage and a passion for vengeance against its creator.

A machine can't appear to have a will of its own unless it is a system, not just a device. It needs parts that interact in unexpected and sometimes unstable and unwanted ways. A flat tire is not a system problem. A failure of battery charging may well be one. Any one of a number of parts of the automobile's circuit, or interactions among them, may be responsible. An individual part may be warranted for thirty days; no electrical system repair is likely to come with any meaningful guarantee. Industrial society did not begin the deceptive sale of an inferior product or an unhealthy animal. Horse traders once had the reputation enjoyed by used-car salespeople today. But there is a difference. The complexity of mechanical systems makes it impossible to test for all possible malfunctions and makes it inevitable that in actual use, some great flaws will appear that were hidden from designers.

From Use to Management

Technology before Mary Shelley's time did not come in systems. Well into the nineteenth century, artisanal tools and farm implements were extensions of the user's mind and body. In Central Europe and no doubt elsewhere, a scythe, for example, was custom-proportioned to the cultivator's body as a suit of clothes might be. Even a large, bureaucratically supervised enterprise like an arsenal or print shop was a complex of craftsmen rather than a factory in the nineteenth- or twentieth-century sense.

As the museum curator James R. Blackaby has pointed out, the link between person and instrument was changing in America on the eve of industrialization. A rough, low bench called a shaving horse was common in colonial America. With a foot-operated clamp, it involved the whole body of the operator. The finer workbench, then already long used by professional artisans, began to displace the shaving horse on the farm in the nineteenth century.

The workbench changed the relationship between the operator's body and the tools. It is a well-finished, solid table for anchoring the material with pegs and vises. The operator usually stands. And above all, the tools have more of the operator's intelligence and skill built into them. Adzes and drawknives demand experience and judgment. Planes have to be mastered, too. Yet once a job is set up right, they make constant judgment and adjustment unnecessary. Even an inexperienced woodworker can cut an elaborate piece by setting up the work and the plane blade properly. Most molding and grooving planes are constructed to cut only to a preadjusted depth. Skill is concentrated more in the conception, setup, and beginning of work than in each successive detail of its execution.

We cease to be tool *users* and, in Blackaby's phrase, begin to be tool *managers*. We direct and control processes that take place rather than shape them. Blackaby has contrasted the leather-cased ivory slide rule presented to him as a college freshman by his father with the electronic calculator he has since come to use. One requires human judgment, experience, and the constant exercise of skill; the other simply executes the operations it is programmed to do.

The calculator is in principle accurate to several more decimal places than the slide rule, but it is so only as long as its solid-state and mechanical parts are interacting properly. And there may be no clue when they are not. I once discovered—at tax time, of course—that an electronic printing calculator I had bought was starting to get its sums wrong. The problem was almost certainly in the print wheel advance mechanisms, but the tapes showed no sign of it. They looked impeccable until I saw that the numbers did not add up. Unlike a mechanical adding machine, my calculator did not merely malfunction; it gave dangerously wrong readings without a clue. The precision of the managed tool has a price. It may be less robust and, as it becomes more complex, less predictable.

Frankenstein Warns of the Perils of Promethean Science

M.K. Joseph

M.K. Joseph was a British-born New Zealand poet and novelist whose works include I'll Soldier No More, A Pound of Saffron, *and* A Soldier's Tale.

Taking his cue from the subtitle of Frankenstein, *which reads or, The Modern Prometheus, Joseph explores in this selection how the Greek myth of the Titan who stole fire from the gods informs our understanding of Mary Shelley's novel. Both her husband, Percy Bysshe Shelley, and their friend Lord Byron had recently written works featuring Prometheus, and she was influenced by these works in her own story. Joseph asserts that while Prometheus is often portrayed as a prototype of the creative artist, Shelley uses the Prometheus myth to suggest the creative nature of the scientific discoveries that were proliferating in Europe in the late eighteenth century. Thus Shelley's Promethean rebel, Victor Frankenstein, serves as a symbol of the dangers of scientific Prometheanism.*

When Mary Wollstonecraft Godwin began to write *Frankenstein*, she was not quite nineteen; yet none of her later novels has achieved anything like the same universal hold on the imagination. Whatever she may have owed to other novelists, particularly to her father William Godwin and to the American Charles Brockden Brown, the novel remains completely original. In spite of her errors, which are those of a novice—particularly her tendency to invent fresh improbabilities rather than to think her way through difficult passages in the story—the central idea is carried through with considerable skill and force.

M.K. Joseph, *Frankenstein; or the Modern Prometheus*. Oxford: Oxford University Press, 2008. Editorial matter copyright © 1952 Oxford University Press. Reproduced by permission of Oxford University Press.

The unexpected and bizarre success of the novel was due to one of those lucky accidents which, in most writers' lives, happen only once. For two troubled and uncertain years, she had been living with [English poet Percy Bysshe] Shelley. Now, in the summer of 1816, they had temporarily escaped from England and were settled in Geneva, [Switzerland,] among the splendours of lake and mountains, and in the stimulating company of [English poet George Gordon, Lord] Byron. The germ of *Frankenstein* is to be found somewhere in their wide-ranging nightly conversations, which must have covered, not only gothic terrors and galvanism and current theories on the origin of life, but also the myth of Prometheus and its significance. For Mary subtitled her story 'the modern Prometheus', and this is an essential clue to its meaning.

Elements of the Prometheus Myth

The myth of Prometheus contains two main elements. The first, best known through the [play] *Prometheus Bound* of [ancient Greek playwright] Aeschylus, was the story of Prometheus *pyrphoros* [the fire bringer], who had brought down fire from the sun in order to succour mankind, and whom Zeus had punished by chaining him to the Caucasus [Mountains in Eurasia] with an eagle feeding on his vitals. The second was the story of Prometheus *plasticator* [shaper] who, in some versions, was said to have created or recreated mankind by animating a figure made of clay. This aspect of the myth, little used by the Greeks and unknown to Aeschylus or [Greek poet] Hesiod, seems to have been more popular with the Romans.

By about the second or third century A.D., the two elements were fused together, so that the fire stolen by Prometheus was also the fire of life with which he animated his man of clay. This gave a radically new significance to the myth which lent itself easily to Neoplatonic interpretation [after the philosophy of classical Greek philosopher Plato] with

Prometheus as the demiurge [a powerful creative force] or deputy creator, but which could also be readily allegorized by Christians and was frequently used in the Middle Ages as a representation of the creative power of God. By the Renaissance, the image was a familiar one, as in Othello's words over Desdemona [in Shakespeare's play *Othello*]:

> ... I know not where is that Promethean heat

> That can thy light relume.

Later still, Prometheus became an accepted image of the creative artist. Early in the eighteenth century a convenient and influential account of Prometheus the creator is to be found in [British writer Anthony Ashley Cooper, Earl of] Shaftesbury's [philosophical treatise] *Characteristicks* [*of Men, Manners, Opinions, Times*], which exactly suggests the central ideas and situations in *Frankenstein*, whether or not Mary had firsthand knowledge of the *Characteristicks* at the time she wrote the novel.

Before 1816 Shelley seems to have been unaware of the potent symbolic significance of the myth; it was Byron, to whom Prometheus had been a familiar figure ever since he translated a portion of Aeschylus while still a schoolboy at Harrow, who opened his eyes to its potentialities during that summer at Geneva. That it was discussed at the time can be inferred from the results: Byron's poem, 'Prometheus', written in July 1816; his *Manfred*, with its Promethean hero, begun in September; and [Percy] Shelley's *Prometheus Unbound*, in part a reply to *Manfred*, begun later in 1818. But Mary Shelley was first in the field with her 'modern Prometheus', and she alone seized on the vital significance of making Prometheus the creator rather than, as in Byron and Shelley, the suffering champion of mankind. In doing so, she linked the myth with certain current scientific theories which suggested that the 'divine spark' of life might be electrical or quasi-electrical in nature.

Science in *Frankenstein*

In the novel itself, Victor Frankenstein is understandably reluctant to reveal how he gave life to his creature; but there are clues to what Mary Shelley had in mind. In her Introduction she recalls the talk about [English physician] Erasmus Darwin, who had 'preserved a piece of vermicelli [pasta] in a glass case, till by some extraordinary means it began to move with voluntary motion'; but this sounds like an ordinary case of alleged spontaneous generation. 'Not thus, after all, would life be given. Perhaps a corpse would be re-animated; galvanism had given token of such things: perhaps the component parts of a creature might be manufactured, brought together, and endued with vital warmth.' She then goes on to describe the half-waking reverie which gave her the beginning of her story, in which 'I saw the hideous phantasm of a man stretched out, and then, on the working of some powerful engine, show signs of life, and stir with an uneasy, half vital motion.' Nor is the story itself without hints: in Chapter II a discourse on electricity and magnetism—the point is more explicit in *1818*—turns Frankenstein's mind away from alchemy; and in Chapter V the 'instruments of life' which Frankenstein assembles before infusing the 'spark of life' also suggest an electrical rather than a biological process.

Frankenstein's change of interest from alchemy to chemistry and electricity is a circumstance obviously drawn from Shelley himself; and with the mention of electricity as vitalizing force we come, as [literary critic] Carl Grabo has shown, to a central idea of Shelley's which was to emerge, a little later, in the last act of *Prometheus Unbound*. In his eclectic synthesis of ideas drawn from [English scientist Sir Isaac] Newton, [Italian physicist] Volta, [Italian physician and physicist] Galvani, Erasmus Darwin, and [English scientist] Humphry Davy (whom Mary was reading in October 1816), electricity became the divine fire, the life-principle, and the physical manifestation of spiritual love—of which [literary critic] Douglas

Bush remarks: '[English philosopher Bishop George] Berkeley and Newton are met together, [Greek philosopher] Plotinus and [American inventor Thomas Alva] Edison have kissed each other.' It seems likely that, during the conversations at [Byron's Villa] Diodati, Mary absorbed from Shelley—and perhaps from [Byron's physician John] Polidori as well—the idea of making electricity the animating force, the scientific equivalent of that divine spark which, in the myth, Prometheus had stolen from the sun.

The Structure of *Frankenstein*

Frankenstein is constructed of three concentric layers, one within the other. In the outermost layer, Robert Walton, in his letters to his sister, describes his voyage towards the North Pole and his encounter with Victor Frankenstein. In the main, middle layer, Frankenstein tells Walton how he created the monster and abandoned it in disgust, how it revenged itself by murdering all those he loved and how he finally turned and pursued it. In the very centre, the monster himself describes the development of his mind after the flight from the laboratory and his bitterness when men reject him. In spite of her inexperience, Mary Shelley uses this concentric structure with considerable subtlety.

The story of Walton's voyage to the Pole is strange but possible; it mediates by interposing a conceivable reality between us and the more strictly marvellous story of Frankenstein and his monster, which thus remains doubly insulated from everyday reality. Yet there is a parallelism of situation and a strong bond of sympathy between Walton and Frankenstein which they are quick to recognize. Walton is a solitary like Frankenstein and his obsession with the Pole answers to Frankenstein's obsession with life. Sharing something of Frankenstein's Faustian [referring to the dramatic character Dr. Faustus, or Faust, who sold his soul to the devil] *hybris* [excessive pride], Walton is setting out on a process of scien-

Mary Shelley's Frankenstein *was inspired by the Greek myth of Prometheus, a Titan who stole fire from the gods to animate the man he had crafted out of clay.* © Bettmann/Corbis.

tific discovery at great peril to himself and others. Frankenstein's story is, in fact, narrated as a cautionary tale which serves its purpose in the end by turning Walton back to the world of normal society. At the same time, Walton's voyage through the Frozen Sea towards the Pole, with its conscious echoes of [English poet Samuel Taylor Coleridge's] 'The Ancient Mariner', reflects that other world of the Mer de Glace at Chamonix [glacier in the Alps], the setting in which the monster tells his story to Frankenstein.

At the centre of the triple structure is the story of the education of a natural man and of his dealings with his creator, which might be described (with important reservations) as a sort of Godwinian Genesis [a creation myth modeled on the work of Mary Shelley's father]. The theme is stated plainly at the beginning of the monster's conversation with his maker:

> Remember, that I am thy creature; I ought to be thy Adam; but I am rather the fallen angel, whom thou drivest from joy for no misdeed. Every where I see bliss, from which I alone am irrevocably excluded. I was benevolent and good; misery made me a fiend. Make me happy, and I shall again be virtuous.

The monster is essentially benevolent; but rejection by his creator and by mankind at large has made him first a fallen Adam [of the Book of Genesis] and then a fallen Lucifer [an angel, sometimes identified with Satan].

In the story of his experiences there are certain improbabilities and some rather obvious contrivance—the convenient chink in the wall of De Lacey's cottage, the providentially lost portmanteau [trunk] of books, the lessons to the Arab girl Safie which also serve to provide the eavesdropping monster with a kind of crash-course in European civilization. These can be more easily forgiven if we take it that here, in the centre of the book, Mary Shelley is constructing something with the schematic character of a philosophic romance. The story of the monster's beginnings is the story of a child, and at the same time he recapitulates the development of aboriginal man. He awakes to the world of the senses, discovers fire and searches for food. When men reject him, he discovers society by watching the De Laceys in their cottage. Having thus acquired language, from Felix's reading of [Count] Volney he learns of human history; having learned to read, he discovers private sentiment in [German writer Johann Wolfgang von Goethe's] *Werther* and public virtue in [Greek historian] Plutarch.

Creator and Creation

Most of all, it is through [English poet John Milton's] *Paradise Lost* that he comes to understand himself and his situation under the double analogy of Adam and of Satan. At the same time, through the copy of Frankenstein's journal which he has conveniently carried off in his first flight from the laboratory, he learns that his situation is yet more desperate than theirs, since he has been rejected without guilt and is utterly companionless. 'I am malicious because I am miserable'; it is this that turns him against his maker and against mankind. What he demands, not unreasonably, is to be supplied with an Eve of his own hideous kind and to return to the natural life, with 'the vast wilds of South America' for his Eden.

Frankenstein is moved to pity; it is only when he revolts and destroys his second, half-formed creature that the monster finally becomes a fallen angel, a Satan bent on mischief, as he acknowledges at the end, over the dead body of Frankenstein. 'Evil thenceforth became my good,' he says, again recalling Milton; '. . . the fallen angel becomes a malignant devil'. His final suicide by burning at the North Pole will reconcile the novel's central images of fire and ice, of life and desolation, of Promethean heat and the frosty Caucasus.

Yet Frankenstein himself is also both a fallen Adam and a fallen Lucifer: '. . . the apple was already eaten, and the angel's arm bared to drive me from all hope'; '. . . like the archangel who aspired to omnipotence, I am chained in an eternal hell'. There is a strict parallel between the role of each in his own story, and we are drawn to complete the equation for ourselves: as the monster is to Frankenstein, so perhaps is Frankenstein to whatever power created man. The clue to the monster's predicament—benevolence corrupted—may also be the clue to Frankenstein's.

Frankenstein disowns but cannot free himself from his monster, which thus takes on the character of a *doppel-gänger* [double] or a Mr. Hyde [Dr. Jekyll's evil alter ego in Robert Louis Stevenson's novel]. Their interdependence is evoked with considerable power in the last part of Frankenstein's narrative in which Frankenstein, from being the pursued, becomes the pursuer; yet, by a sort of complicity, he is also lured on willingly by the monster across the snowbound landscape of Russia, in an atmosphere of dream and delirium, towards the Frozen Sea. It is, in fact, only at the very end of the book, when Walton encounters the monster grieving over Frankenstein's body, that we can at last be quite sure that the whole story is 'true' and not a madman's hallucination. Yet the monster is, in a literal sense, a projection of Frankenstein's and an embodiment of his guilt in withdrawing from his kind and pursuing knowledge which, though not forbidden, is still dangerous. He is also a reflection of Frankenstein's own situation, and the quotation from *Paradise Lost* which appeared on the original title-page—the accusing words of fallen Adam to his creator—might apply to both:

> Did I request thee, Maker, from my clay
>
> To mould me Man? did I solicit thee
>
> From darkness to promote me?

The implications of Mary Shelley's 'ghost-story' go much further than she or any of her circle seem to have understood, though there are hints of uneasiness in Shelley's Preface of 1817. With unassuming originality, her 'modern Prometheus' challenges the whole myth of Romantic titanism, of Shelley's Neoplatonic apocalypse in *Prometheus Unbound*, and of the artist as Promethean creator. One of its themes is solitude— the solitude of one who turns his back on his kind in his obsessive pursuit of the secrets of nature. Frankenstein sins against the Godwinian ideal of social benevolence; in describing him, Mary probably had in mind the proem [preface] to [Percy] Shelley's [poem] *Alastor, or the Spirit of Solitude*, in which he described his own vigils in the charnel-house:

> Like an inspired and desperate alchymist
>
> Staking his very life on some dark hope . . .

Scientific Prometheanism

Prometheus was also an accepted metaphor of the artist, but when Mary Shelley transfers this to the scientist, the implications are radical. If Frankenstein, as scientist, is 'the modern Prometheus', then science too is creative; but whereas the world of art is ideal and speculative, that of science is real and inescapable. It must then take the consequences: the scientist, himself a creature, has taken on the role and burden of a creator. If Frankenstein corrupts the monster by his rejection, which is good Godwinism so far, we are left asking a question which demands another kind of answer: what has rejected and corrupted Frankenstein? And if Prometheus, in the romantic tradition, is identified with human revolt, is the monster what that revolt looks like from the other side—a pitiful botched-up creature, a 'filthy mass that moved and talked', which brings nothing but grief and destruction upon the power that made him?

Mary Shelley wrote in the infancy of modern science, when its enormous possibilities were just beginning to be foreseen by imaginative writers like Byron and Shelley and by speculative scientists like Davy and Erasmus Darwin. At the age of nineteen, she achieved the quietly astonishing feat of looking beyond them and creating a lasting symbol of the perils of scientific Prometheanism. Her success is shown by the simple fact that her tale has acquired a kind of independent mythic life.

Contemporary
Perspectives on Bioethics

Transplant Surgeons Must Determine When an Organ Donor Is Truly Dead

Kevin B. O'Reilly

Kevin B. O'Reilly covers medical ethics, patient safety, and health care quality improvement for the American Medical Association's American Medical News.

In the following viewpoint O'Reilly writes that when it comes to pediatric organ transplants, determining exactly when a donor has died is becoming a critical issue. The sooner organs are taken from the donor and given to a patient in need, he reports, the better the chances of success. But many ethicists argue that it is critical to wait until the donor has truly died before taking the organs, asserts the author. The "dead donor rule," adopted in all fifty U.S. states, deems that patients must be declared irreversibly dead before vital organs can be taken for transplant. But definitions of "irreversibly dead" vary from hospital to hospital. In his discussions with experts, O'Reilly finds that more definitive guidelines are needed in an area where definitions are a matter of life and death.

A days-old infant sustained severe neurological injury after being asphyxiated during birth, but the dying baby's condition did not meet the criteria for brain death—long the only circumstance under which vital organs were procured. The baby was transferred to Children's Hospital in Aurora, Colo., a suburb of Denver, where the family decided to withdraw life support. Family members also agreed to let surgeons there attempt to transplant the baby's heart into an infant born with complex congenital heart disease.

Waiting for Death

But to accomplish this, the potential donor heart had to stop working. The question: How long after cardiac functioning ceased should the retrieval team wait to ensure the baby's heart would not restart without intervention? The complicating factors: Odds of successful transplantation decrease as the wait after cessation of cardiocirculatory function increases. But acting too soon can make retrieval seem like death by organ donation.

The Denver team waited 75 seconds.

The infant who received that heart lived, as did two other babies who received hearts from donations retrieved shortly after cardiac death in transplants the Denver team performed between May 2004 and May 2007. The results were published in the Aug. 14, 2008, *New England Journal of Medicine* [*NEJM*].

The clinical debate over whether 75 seconds without cardiac function after withdrawing life support is sufficient time to confidently declare death is unsettled, but the questions these cases raise go even deeper. Some bioethicists and physicians say the cases are merely the latest in the organ transplantation era to stretch the definition of death in ways that could potentially undermine Americans' trust in physicians and in the organ donation process.

Expanding the pool of potential pediatric heart donors beyond those who meet brain-death criteria can help meet a pressing need. About 100 infants younger than a year old receive life-saving heart transplants every year. But as many as 50 infants in need of heart transplants die each year while waiting on the United Network for Organ Sharing list, according to an *NEJM* editorial.

About a third of infants who die in pediatric hospitals do so after life support is withdrawn. These infants represent a valuable pool of life-saving organs. The Denver team said that at Children's Hospital, 12 potential infant donors died of cardiocirculatory causes during the three years of the study, accounting for a possible 70% increase in organ donation.

According to the "dead-donor rule" adopted as law in all 50 states, patients must be declared irreversibly dead before their vital organs can be retrieved for transplantation, provided there is consent from patients or surrogate decision-makers.

Securing organs from brain-dead patients has been deemed ethical since a Harvard Medical School committee formulated the criteria in 1968; every state recognizes brain death as legal death.

Over the last decade and a half organ donation after cardiac death has become medically and legally acceptable, though the timing question has proved contentious. The so-called Pittsburgh protocol, published in 1993, called for a two-minute wait after cardiopulmonary arrest before declaring death and retrieving organs. The Institute of Medicine [IOM] in 1997 said transplant teams should wait five minutes after cardiac functioning ceases before retrieving organs.

Then in 2000, the IOM said some data suggested a shorter interval of 60 seconds, though its report said "existing empirical data cannot confirm or disprove a specific interval at which the cessation of cardiopulmonary function becomes irreversible." The Society of Critical Care Medicine recommends a wait of at least two minutes but no longer than five minutes.

American Medical Association policy doesn't address the time issue, but says the practice is "ethically acceptable" as long as conflict-of-interest and palliative care protocols are followed.

In its first infant heart donor case, the Colorado team waited three minutes. But the Children's Hospital ethics committee determined, based on data it reviewed, that a 75-second wait would be sufficient and would reduce the risk of injury to the donor heart from blood loss.

Debating How Long to Wait

This groundbreaking decision has received fierce criticism, including a series of editorials published in the *NEJM*. A member of the Children's Hospital ethics committee declined to speak with *AMNews* [*American Medical News*].

But the author of one editorial derided as "arbitrary" the 75-second protocol the Colorado team used. "We know that infants, compared to older people, tend to be more resilient," said James L. Bernat, MD, professor of medicine and neurology at the Dartmouth Medical School in New Hampshire. "We are always more conservative in our delineations with infants. It's especially troubling that they reached that conclusion."

The process of deciding how long to wait before declaring cardiac death "shouldn't be done ad hoc," he said. "It should be something done following guidelines. There are some guidelines out there; admittedly, there could be better ones. I understand why they wanted to shorten the wait, but I don't think it's a good idea."

Bioethicist Arthur L. Caplan, PhD, agreed. "I'm not against moving fast and saving other lives. But the big 'but' is you have to do that with a national consensus, not local groups saying when it comes to neonates 75 seconds is plenty of time to wait," said Caplan, director of the University of Pennsylvania Center for Bioethics.

Other critics said the concept of transplanting a heart after cardiac death isn't logical.

"If someone is pronounced dead on the basis of irreversible loss of heart function, after all, it would not be possible for heart function to be restored in another body," wrote Robert M. Veatch, PhD, a Georgetown University medical ethics professor, in an Aug. 14, 2008, *NEJM* essay. "One cannot say a heart is irreversibly stopped if, in fact, it will be restarted."

Veatch said the dead-donor rule should be changed to allow patients or their families to opt for a standard that takes a

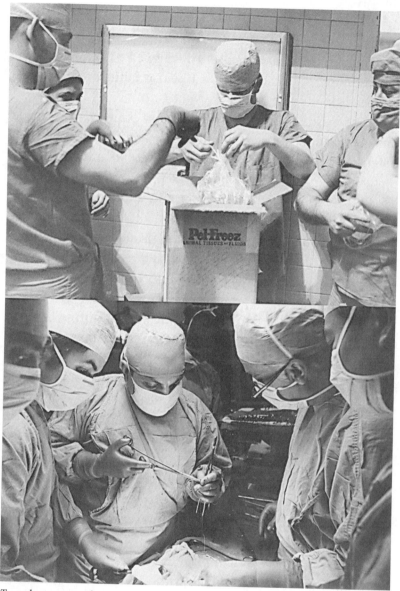

Transplant surgeons face a moral dilemma—they are required to determine when an organ donor is truly dead. © Bettmann/Corbis.

loss of functioning consciousness (short of brain death) as another kind of death. Physicians could then procure hearts "in the absence of irreversible heart stoppage."

Various Definitions of Death

Robert D. Truog, MD, said the Denver cases illustrate the underlying problem in how death is defined to facilitate organ donation and transplantation. He said it is time to reconsider the dead-donor rule.

"The existing paradigm, built around the dead-donor rule, has increasingly pushed us into more and more implausible definitions of death, until eventually we end up with such a tortured definition that nobody's going to believe it," said Dr. Truog, professor of medical ethics and anesthesia at Harvard Medical School in Massachusetts.

"When you get there, you run the risk of really undermining confidence in what this whole system is about," he said.

"We are seeing it play out in the Denver example," he added. "What made it problematic was that they were trying to fit what they did into our existing ethical norms. It's like trying to fit square pegs in round holes. It just doesn't fit."

Dr. Truog has long argued for what he admits is a "radical departure" from the current definition of norms for death. He disagrees that brain death is actual death, noting that major life functions continue. Brain-dead patients have given birth, for example.

Dr. Truog argues that vital organ donation does cause patients to die, and to say otherwise misleads patients and families. But dying patients on life support and their families have a right to consent to such donations, even if it causes death, he said.

While the debate over the timing of cardiac death is contentious, most experts disagree with Dr. Truog's opinion on the dead-donor role.

"The dead-donor rule serves a great purpose," said John J. Paris, a Boston College bioethicist. "There is a great sentiment among people that [physicians] might try to do you in to take your organs. . . . The protection is we only take organs from those who are dead and can't take organs to cause them to be dead, which is a substantial leap from where we are. And the slippery slope is very slippery in that case. If you don't have to be dead to get the organs, then from whom can we take them?"

Dr. Truog said no transplants should take place without consent from patients or their surrogates, and such donations should be limited to patients whose surrogates want to discontinue life support.

That standard is not good enough for Georgetown's Veatch.

He said Dr. Truog's proposal "amounts to an endorsement of active, intentional killing of the patient—that is, active euthanasia. It would be euthanasia by vital organ removal."

The Denver heart transplant cases already have sparked a contentious debate over how soon is too soon to declare death. Whether physicians, bioethicists and lawmakers will be spurred to redefine death remains to be seen.

Franklin G. Miller, PhD, said it is unlikely. He has co-authored articles with Dr. Truog that call for doing away with the dead-donor rule.

He predicted that "we can just muddle through" with the current definitions of death.

Miller, a bioethicist at the National Institutes of Health, said "people will get bent out of shape" by critiques of the dead-donor rule. "But I think we need, in a way, to get bent out of shape to make sense out of what we're already doing."

The Sale of Body Parts Should Be Legalized

Gary Jason

Gary Jason writes for Liberty, *a libertarian journal of culture and politics. He is also a businessman and philosophy instructor in southern California.*

The U.S. government has banned the sale of human organs. But legalizing body part sales has its benefits, contends Jason in this viewpoint, especially in an era when donations are not adequate to fill the ever-increasing need for transplants to those who are gravely ill. It has been estimated that every day seventeen Americans die waiting for organ donations that never materialize. Jason argues that the tightly regulated selling of human body parts may have utilitarian validity, despite the current government taboo. Certainly there are risks of abuse in any cash-for-body-parts program, he asserts, but the growing need for human organs suggests that more practical and less idealistic laws are needed.

The federal government prohibits the sale (as opposed to the donation) of human organs. Under the National Organ Transplant Act of 1984 (NOTA), it is a felony to give or receive compensation for them. Legalizing sales has been discussed in some circles, but proposals to let people sell their own organs as they see fit do not appear at the top of the list of most discussed issues, or anywhere close to the top.

Yet the issue of organ sales (sales of body parts, bone, skin, and tissues of any sort) is becoming ever more urgent. One reason has been noted by [journalist] Laura Meckler: for many years, organ transplants were rare, dangerous, and costly, and the supply of donated organs from the deceased was

Gary Jason, "The Market for Body Parts," *Liberty*, vol. 21, October 2007, pp. 33–36.

enough to cover demand. But now that organ transplants are relatively routine, relatively safe, and covered by many insurance plans, the number of organs available from donor corpses is insufficient. Patients either have to wait or turn to living relatives for donations.

The problem will become more dramatically evident over the next decade, when for the first time in our history elderly people will be upwards of a third of our population. And the notoriously narcissistic Baby Boomers will hardly be squeamish about replacing their faulty organs. Look how many have embraced Botox injections and cosmetic surgery, procedures that have nothing to do with keeping you alive.

A Proposal Worthy of Discussion

So the proposal to legalize organ sales is well worth discussing—but with some care.

Certainly, from the libertarian perspective [a philosophy advocating individual liberty] there is a compelling moral case for it. Being a free agent means that I control my own body. If my body isn't my property, what is? The idea goes back to one of the founding documents of libertarianism, [English philosopher] John Locke's "Second Treatise on government." Even if you draw the line at suicide, as Locke did, selling a kidney won't kill you, at least in normal cases. This is all the more true if we are talking about my agreeing *while alive* to sell any kidneys *after I am dead*. Another idea that has been influential on libertarianism, the harm principle, enunciated very clearly by John Stuart Mill, tells us that rational people ought to be allowed to do whatever they please, so long as it doesn't harm anyone else. Well, what harm is done to anyone else if I decide to sell Fred one of my kidneys? *Prima facie* [at first sight], there doesn't seem to be any—indeed, it will likely save Fred's life.

Utilitarian ideas [which suggest that the end justifies the means] also seem favorable. If I benefit from the money Fred pays me for my kidney, and he is better off, then everyone directly affected by my action benefits. As a rule, allowing organ sales would increase the wealth of the poorer and the longevity of the wealthier. It would obviously encourage more donations of life-giving organs. Consider how many more people would put codicils [additions] in their wills allowing the extraction of their body parts upon their demise if the sales money could be passed along to surviving spouses and other heirs.

If the philosophical case seems defensible, add to it a reason drawn from precedent and current practice. People are free to sell their blood, and many regularly supplement their income by doing so. And people are free *to donate* their body parts. If people are rationally capable of and morally entitled to give away their body parts, why can't they profit by the transaction? That is, if my autonomy as a thinking, choosing human being allows me to grasp the risk and pain of an operation to give a kidney to my child because I love her, then why not allow me to sell my kidney to a stranger, for love of money? Remember that money is typically desired instrumentally, as a tool to get other things; it is seldom loved intrinsically, for itself. Suppose that the money I get from selling my kidney will be used to help my family—give them, say, better food, or a better house, or a better education. Is that not also a case of giving my kidney to save my family, albeit indirectly?

Benefits of Organ Sales

Now consider the practical benefits of organ sales. One of the most important of them is that it addresses the shortage of organs available for transplant. Meckler puts the number of living *donors* (usually kidney donors) at about 7,000 a year. Most of them are people who give organs to keep family members alive. Those willing to donate to strangers are much more limited. Several internet sites have been developed to make it easy for willing donors to connect with those who need organs; *MatchingDonors.com* is one example. But the last I checked, there were fewer than 4,000 such persons. This is woefully inadequate. One recent estimate is that there are over 90,000 Americans already waiting for body parts. Other estimates are of 70,000 waiting for kidney transplants alone. The shortage has several consequences.

To begin with: people die. A few years ago, Brian Doherty estimated that every day, 17 Americans die waiting for organs. No doubt the figure is higher now. The shortage has also created a black market, with all the unpleasant side effects that brings. There have been cases in which people have purchased organs of uncertain provenance, only to find out that they were taken from people who died of syphilis or hepatitis B. Finally, the shortage has produced the bizarre result, nicely explored by Kerry Howley, that in this black market, everyone pockets good money except the donors. This is extremely unfair compensation.

Why, then, would anyone object to organ sales? There are three broad reasons: first, worries by medical ethicists about the nature of the choice; second, concerns about the potential for abuse, as suggested by some recent horrific headlines; and third, concerns raised by some religious ethicists about the sanctity of the human body. Let me briefly examine these areas of concern.

Objections to Organ Sales

You can get an idea of what troubles medical ethicists by looking at an article by Thomas Papadimos and Alexa Papadimos that opposes allowing women to sell their ova to pay their college tuition. The Papadimos paper raises a number of objections to the practice, objections that apply equally well if not more forcefully to organ sales in general. Ironically, all the objections are considerations of autonomy.

The authors view autonomy as involving "voluntariness, competence, capacity, understanding, and disclosure. . . ." And they feel that decisions to sell ova fail to meet the standards of real autonomy. One of their arguments is that, since college students need the money, they are under the influence of the buyers. They are being exploited. Another argument is that the age of the students (typically, 20–25) makes their mental capacity questionable, and renders suspect their ability to understand risks. As the authors put it, "Persons may comprehend information, but do not or cannot accept the information. For example, if a twenty year old female is told she has a 1% chance of hemorrhaging, a 1% chance of having a post operative infection, and a remote chance of death with an egg donation procedure; can she accept this? Can she understand the long-term risk of fertility drugs, including the risk of cancer? This young woman may very well understand these risks, but can she actually accept the fact that she has a remote, yet possible chance of getting cancer or dying?"

These theoretical worries strike me as hyperbolic. Again, look at actual practice. We allow young women to take birth control pills and elect for surgery of all sorts, from abortion to cosmetic surgery. All involve significant risk. We allow young men and women to drive cars, not to mention volunteer for combat; this also involves significant risk, and with far less disclosure required. As to the idea that the need for money invalidates a person's autonomy, that would seem to disallow any trade of any sort in any economic realm.

Turning next to the potential for abuse of a free market in organs, recent horrific headlines suggest major problems. There have been cases of sophisticated grave-robbing. A recent New York case is illustrative. Seven funeral home directors pleaded guilty to plundering corpses for body parts. They removed bone, skin, and organs from hundreds of corpses, pocketing millions by selling the tissues to biomed companies. A recent AP [Associated Press] report announced the apprehension of a former director of UCLA's [University of California, Los Angeles] Willed Body Program. He was arrested for appropriating parts of the bodies donated for research and selling them to an outside company for tens of thousands of dollars. The owner of the company was also arrested; he had made over a million dollars by reselling those body parts to various hospitals and medical research companies.

Chinese Abuses

News stories have also been generated by the aggressive harvesting of organs by certain authoritarian regimes, most notoriously China. Recent stories . . . indicate that the Chinese are systematically harvesting organs from executed prisoners and selling them to rich Japanese and Americans, who pay about $50,000 per kidney and $110,000 per liver. This is a significant inflow of foreign currency to a country that executes 8,000 people yearly, more than all other countries combined. Even more ominous are recent reports that China now targets groups it dislikes, such as political dissidents and Falun Gong [dissident Chinese group] for arrest and execution, in part because the trade in human organs is so lucrative. Even more alarming are reports that the organs are being harvested from prisoners who are still alive.

The Chinese government heatedly denies these various reports. China's foreign ministry has conceded using some organs from prisoners, but only with prior permission. Its spokesman, Qin Gang, said, "It is a complete falsification, a lie or slander to say that China forcibly takes organs from the people convicted of the death penalty for the purpose of transplanting them." Still, China has announced it will start requiring donors to give permission in writing before allowing transplants. This is the same government that denies it has carried out any military buildup, that Tibet was ever an independent nation, and that anyone died at Tiananmen Square [during the 1989 student uprising]. Its credibility is hardly compelling. But in any case, the danger is clear: allowing an unrestricted market in organs runs the risk of giving incentives to totalitarian regimes to violate people's rights in the most horrible ways. From a tyrannical government's psychopathic point of view, it's a perfect "two-fer": it gets rid of annoying groups *and* makes a ton of money.

But it is easy to draw the wrong conclusion from such claims. I would argue that what is driving people to go to totalitarian regimes or other black markets is precisely the growing unmet demand for organs by people who face certain death if they don't get them. If you don't let these people obtain what they need legally, don't be surprised when they do so illegally.

Sacredness of the Body

The third set of concerns—those of religious ethicists—centers on feelings that the body is sacred, not to be tampered with lightly or for base motives. Some people suspect that legalizing organ sales will somehow be like legalizing abortions; it will cheapen life and encourage an ungodly practice.

Again, I find such worries understandable but overblown. There is little comparison between abortion, the killing of a new life-form, and selling an organ, which is someone's existing tissue, for the purpose of moving it to another's body. While many religions hold that the fetus has a soul (at some point in its development), no religion of which I have ever heard views my liver as having a soul. Moreover, abortion is not generally done to save someone's life, whereas that is the whole point of organ transplants.

In any event, why would giving some of your body to save someone else's life defile your body? And if giving it wouldn't defile your body, why would selling it? Even if one believes that giving tissues defiles his body, what gives him the right to impose that view on others who don't share it—and in so doing, condemn many others to early deaths?

Practical Problems for Organ Sales

While I find the three broad types of concern generally unpersuasive, and the theoretical, practical, and moral case for allowing a free market in organs compelling, there are some legitimate issues that must be addressed—in other words, practical problems that must be addressed by some legal mechanism.

One set of problems involves fraud and misrepresentation. If we are going to allow rational people to sell parts of their bodies, there has to be real informed consent. Downplaying the risk and pain would be an attractive ploy for any sales agent: "Look, kid, what's your worry? You have two kidneys, so you won't even miss one of them. We'll pop it out of you—no hassle! Just think of all the cool stuff you can buy with the ten grand we're giving you?"

Another set of problems involves the limits of people's rationality. The reason we wouldn't want to allow a 12-year-old to sell one of her kidneys is the same reason we don't allow her to drink or have sex: adolescents are not fully capable of making such choices. But what about cases that aren't so clear? What about drug addicts, or the clinically depressed, or people with early Alzheimer's? We need more than a simple age limit here.

Even more worrisome, in my view, are problems of coercion, problems involving people who are executed to harvest their organs, or have their organs stolen after death. Of course, it seems likely that if we were to allow *legal* sales of body parts, the illegal sales would be less attractive, since the price would drop. But we still need appropriate safeguards to minimize the chances of theft, fraud, manipulation, and coercion.

Free Trade with Restrictions

My proposal is to allow free trade in organs, with certain tight restrictions. We should begin by requiring that all purchases of body parts be from sellers who are United States citizens.

The market could be expanded to sellers from other countries, but only on a case-by-case basis, and only when we can assure ourselves that the country in which the sellers live is free and has the same controls on the organ trade that we do. And in exchange for seeing legal organ sales within this country, citizens ought to be willing to prohibit fellow citizens from buying transplants from abroad. That would help stop the kind of abuse going on now, with growing numbers of Americans buying organs from corrupt, totalitarian regimes, where organs are obtained at the cost of liberty.

Second, an organ sale must be accompanied by a contract between the buyer and a named seller, be it an individual or a hospital. This contract would have to be drawn up to legal standards, just like an incorporation or will, by a licensed legal practitioner. And it would have to be accompanied by a sworn affidavit by an independent, licensed medical professional that the seller of the body parts was an adult, apparently of sound mind, and provided blood tests showing him to be free of the influence of drugs or alcohol at the time of signing. At the time of transplantation, the DNA [genetic code] of any purchased body parts should be verified against the DNA of the seller, as listed on the contract.

Third, the contract would have to be accompanied by a signed statement of disclosure, in which the known risks and health consequences of the procedure, as stated by the AMA [American Medical Association] would be listed fully and clearly. The statement would have to be signed by a neutral medical professional, not someone who was a party to the financial transaction. I envision doctors and nurses working *pro bono* [without payment], or being paid by charitable organizations, to apprise sellers of all the consequences of their decisions, without any manipulative sales pitches.

Fourth, when setting age requirements we should distinguish between sales of organs while the seller is still alive from sales of organs after death. Put the minimum age at 18 for the latter (perhaps with special provisions for parents who wish to donate the organs of their deceased child), but 21 for the former.

Fifth, there should be a requirement that any organ available for purchase be checked by a lab for the presence of HIV [human immunodeficiency virus], hepatitis viruses, or other dangerous communicable diseases.

Sixth, the sales of all body parts must be completely recorded and available for inspection on the internet, so that the market will be transparent to all interested parties—potential sellers and potential buyers, as well as journalists and other investigators. In this way, sellers and buyers will know the going price for various body parts, and investigators can monitor sales for patterns of abuse. This will make it less likely that a naive or ignorant person can be tricked into selling his organs at some absurdly low price. We require such transparency for other markets, such as real estate, and the organ market would need it even more.

A Growing Need

There is a clear and growing need for organs and other tissues. Now, there are occasional stories about "cloning organs," i.e., taking a stem cell from a person and growing (say) a replacement liver from it. Of course, were such a procedure to exist, the whole issue of whether we should permit organ sales would be rendered moot—nobody would pay to buy another's organs if he could get new ones based on his own DNA, which would eliminate the problem of tissue rejection and the need for immunosuppressant medications [to mediate the rejection of the foreign organ]. But no such procedure seems even remotely close to becoming available, so our choices remain either keeping organ sales illegal, or making them legal under practical regulation. The case for the second option is far stronger than for the first.

I think there is growing recognition in [government, Washington,] D.C. that something needs to be done soon to solve the shortage of organs created by an ill-considered federal law—Lord, how often do we see the government working at any given time to clean up the damage it caused by its stupid laws of a prior time? Recently, the U.S. House of Representatives passed the Charlie W. Norwood Living Organ Donation Act, which aims to make it easier for donors of kidneys to switch recipients with other donors in cases of biological incompatibility. That is, if I want to donate a kidney to X, and Fred wants to donate a kidney to Y, and my tissue is incompatible with X, but not Y (and vice versa for Fred), the law would allow us to switch recipients. That should result in a fair rise in the number of available kidneys, but it will still be way short of what is needed. We need to open up the process fully and make it transparent, by repealing the NOTA and crafting more realistic and less idealistic laws.

Stem Cell Research Poses Difficult Ethical, Monetary, and Political Issues

John Cornwell

John Cornwell has served as director of the Science and Human Dimension Project at Jesus College in Cambridge, England.

Doctors are developing two main types of stem cells: those extracted from adults and those from embryos. According to Cornwell in the following viewpoint, there is much debate about which type of stem cell offers more promise to help humans live better lives, and many of the arguments, having to do with more than just science, deal with political and monetary issues as well. Because adult stem cells belong to the patient from whom they are harvested, asserts Cornwell, they do not offer the same potential monetary value as embryonic stem cells, which can be patented. Therefore billions of dollars of potential profit are available from embryonic stem cells, even though they raise thornier ethical issues because the embryo is destroyed when the stem cells are removed, and, according to some scientists, they are less promising than adult stem cells. Using the analogy of an unregulated, out-of-control financial sector, Cornwell argues that more oversight is needed to prevent abuses of this emerging technology.

In a biotech laboratory close to the National Hospital for Neurology and Neurosurgery in Bloomsbury, London, Professor Geoffrey Raisman is researching a treatment for spinal cord injury using adult stem cells. This week [in January 2009], with no brief for Republicans or Democrats, he has

John Cornwell, "The Dilemma on the Tip of a Needle: Stem Cell Research May Hold the Key to Future Wonder Cures," *New Statesman*, vol. 138, January 26, 2009, pp. 36–39. Copyright © 2009 New Statesman, Ltd. Reproduced by permission.

been pondering the presidential inauguration celebrations with serious misgivings. He believes that the new president's [Barack Obama's] pledge to fund human embryonic stem cell research could have a detrimental effect on the future of his work.

Embryonic Stem Cells vs. Adult Stem Cells

Ten years ago in a tiny, underequipped laboratory in the University of Wisconsin, Madison, Professor James "Jamie" Thomson, an embryologist, extracted the first human embryonic stem cells from an embryo. Thomson was part of a community of scientists who had been pursuing the "philosopher's stone" of embryonic stem cells with slender resources and huge determination for a decade. Last year [2008], at a conference in New York City calling itself the World Stem Cell Summit, it was projected that the market for stem cell clinical products could reach $8.5bn [billion] within a decade.

Stem cells have potential to be coaxed into different tissue, blood and cell types in the body. In the human embryo they are "totipotent", that is, in a state of greatest potential to become any blood or cell type. But stem cells, albeit with more restricted potential, also exist in adults: in the gut, high in the nose, in blood, in the umbilical cord, and in bone marrow. While stem cell research has been hailed for its prospects for future wonder cures, scientists are divided over the merits of the two basic cell strategies: adult and embryonic. Some, such as Raisman, believe that adult cells are yielding the fastest and safest clinical results; others insist that embryonic cells offer the best prospects. Thus the question arises: where do governments and investors put their money?

Scientists on the Raisman wing believe that human embryonic research holds back medical progress by attracting funds that might otherwise go to adult stem cell work. Raisman, who is not against embryonic stem cell research on ethical grounds, has been funded by the Medical Research Coun-

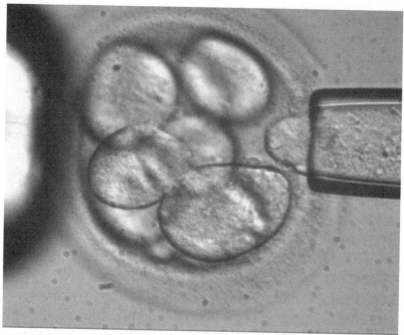

The research of embryonic stem cells raises not only ethical questions, but also monetary and political ones. AP Images.

cil, and by private donations, but in common with many similar research programmes he is underfunded. If President Barack Obama makes good his promise to support funding for human embryonic research, Raisman predicts that there will be a rush to "invest" in embryonic strategy.

Information on the actual sums invested by private industry and governments into the many hundreds of stem cell research programmes worldwide are impossible to calculate because of secrecy. In the meantime, however, adult stem cell therapies have been achieving notable successes. The Stem Cell Summit in New York cited the use of a breast cancer patient's own stem cells in breast reconstruction, and a heart patient whose bone marrow stem cells mended a severe lesion. In Bristol [England], last November, the first tissue-engineered trachea (windpipe), using the patient's own stem cells, were transplanted into a young woman with a failing airway, saving her life. No such tangible successes can yet be produced based on human embryonic stem cells.

Stem Cell Politics

Under George W. Bush, federal funding of human embryonic stem cell work was banned in the United States for religious reasons. Bush's scruples were prompted by the stock objections of the American religious right, which regards human embryos as persons with full human rights. The Catholic Church also bans research that threatens the life of the human embryo for, according to papal teaching reiterated frequently by the late John Paul II, human individuality, or ensoulment, commences from the moment of conception. Research involving embryos has, for two decades, riven churches and religious groups within and outside America, as well as national governmental policies and research communities throughout the west. During his election campaign Obama repeatedly claimed, however, that he would overturn George W. Bush's policy on the issue in the interests of its future benefits for a wide range of illnesses.

Under [British Prime Minister] Tony Blair, Britain adopted a go-ahead policy on human embryonic stem cell research during a period (ending three years back) when the European Union declined to fund such programmes. Last year Britain went beyond the ethical limits of most countries in the west by sanctioning the creation of hybrid animal/human embryos. After a heated nationwide debate, the Human Fertilisation and Embryology Authority (HFEA) licensed three British research laboratories, in Newcastle, London and Warwick, to create embryos in which the ovum comes from an animal (typically a cow or rabbit) and the nuclear DNA [genetic code], from a human being.

The scientific and political arguments in Britain in favour of hybrid embryos focused on the scarcity of donated human embryos available for research, and the claim that such research transgressed moral norms was rejected by parliament. Professor Raisman argues, however, that the ethical debate over both human and hybrid stem cells ignores the issue of intellectual property rights and patenting: in other words, the profit motive. "Adult stem cells are much more promising therapeutically; they are already in use for such things as skin grafting, but they attract less funding and much less interest because they can't be patented." As the adult cells come from the patient's own body, the cells are not amenable to the imposition of intellectual property rights. On the other hand, exploitation of embryonic stem cells for therapy requires many complex laboratory processes from the outset, and is consequently more amenable to patenting. Both governments and industry (principally the pharmaceutical industry) are loath to invest or fund unless they can see the prospect of intellectual property rights—in other words, ownership.

In Britain, consciousness of the urgent requirement to pay heed to patents in medical science gathered impetus when Margaret Thatcher came to power in 1979. She argued that Britain had lost billions of pounds in revenue through a single failure in the mid-1970s to patent an important discovery. The episode, notorious in the annals of British science, involved the development in Cambridge of monoclonal antibodies (crucial to diagnostic testing) by Cesar Millstein's molecular biology team. The discovery was not patented, but a member of the team patented a further development of the process in America, thus earning billions of dollars for biotech research in the United States. During the Thatcher years, the promotion and protection of intellectual property rights in British research became an absolute priority.

Individual European countries have pursued their own national funding policies on embryonic stem cell research, reflecting traditional ethical attitudes, in some cases to the detriment of commercial advantages. While Italy has banned funding because of the influence of the Catholic Church, Germany has been equally reluctant as a consequence of its sensitivity to human experiments in the light of its Nazi history. Japan has adopted similar policies, for the same reasons. Both Germany and Japan invoke the "slippery slope" argument. In other words, they are less preoccupied with doctrinal issues due to their caution based on national historical experience. Britain's more liberal ethical attitudes are largely based on classic utilitarian principles. The ideas of [nineteenth-century political theorists] John Stuart Mill and Jeremy Bentham—the greatest good for the greatest number—hold more sway than arguments about ensouled embryos. When I served on an HFEA inquiry panel two years ago, exploring public attitudes towards hybrid embryos, it was noticeable that the majority of the participants, which included an ordained Church of England ethicist, emphasised the consequentialist clinical benefits—finding cures for Alzheimer's disease, multiple sclerosis, and cancer.

In the United States, the administration's views on stem cell research have been largely shaped by a combination of Evangelical and Catholic attitudes. While Catholics traditionally voted for the Democrats during and after the John F. Kennedy era, the Republicans under George W. Bush's leadership won over a sizeable proportion of the massive Catholic vote. Rights to life, abortion, and embryonic stem cell issues loomed large. A mailshot of four million letters was despatched to Catholics in advance of the 2000 election, claiming that the Republican Party endorsed John Paul II's views on family and life issues. Meanwhile John Kerry, the Democratic candidate, and a Catholic, appeared at odds with his own church on abortion. . . .

The Profit Motive

Professor Raisman is typical of scientists who are agnostic on questions over the status of the human embryo; his jaundiced view of embryonic stem cell research is scientific, he insists.

Using rat models, he has been grafting adult stem cells (known as olfactory ensheathing cells) from the upper region of a rat's nose to create pathways across spinal cord lesions. The strategy has been amazingly successful in rats. Animals that had been paralysed in a front limb have completely regained movement. In the near future, Raisman hopes to apply the treatment to human beings, starting with victims of accidents (typically motorbike riders) who have lost the use of an arm as a result of trauma at a site of the spinal cord known as the brachial plexus (where the shoulder meets the spinal cord). The olfactory human cells will be taken from the patient's own nose, thus reducing the possibility of immunity problems. This is just a prelude to tackling major spinal cord injury.

Raisman complains, however, that he has had scant funding over the years because he cannot promise patents that will make profits. He charges moreover that the media hype for embryonic research as a coming miracle cure, including for spinal cord injury, has put his kind of research programme in the shade. A new surge in government-funded human embryonic research in the United States, he believes, is likely to make things worse, as grant bodies in Britain and elsewhere will seek to compete. "The scramble to fund human embryonic stem cell experiments looks like the scientific equivalent of sub-prime mortgages," says Raisman. "One wonders how long the large sums of money and hype can go on chasing such a distant goal before the bubble bursts."

Many clinicians agree with Raisman that actual therapies using embryonic stem cells are far off. Professor Keith Peters, until recently president of the Academy of Medical Sciences, puts it as distant as two, even three decades. Yet by no means all supporters of embryonic research base their enthusiasm on early delivery of therapies, or on the prospect of financial returns. There are many potential problems with all stem cell therapies, including adult stem cells, as scientists such as Raisman agree. Scientists still do not know how to make embryonic stem cells proliferate reliably, or indeed switch off once they do proliferate; hence there is anxiety that cancers could develop in treated patients.

All the more reason, according to one constituency of the research lobby, for studying human stem cells from their very earliest stage: the embryo. Most persuasive on this score is Professor James Pedersen of Cambridge University (who came to Britain from San Francisco to escape Bush's ban on federal funding in 2004). He argues that reliable stem cell therapies must go hand in hand with fundamental research on the process of development from conception to birth to understand in depth how stem cells work, and hence how to avoid mistakes in therapies. Pedersen's largely academic, non-clinical developmental work, however, does not involve the scramble for patenting rights described by Professor Raisman.

The Need for Regulation

While the scientific row over funding and patenting heats up against the background of the new American president's science policies, the ethical arguments are likely to be revived in a population where 57 percent believe in creationism: the literal belief in the Genesis creation story. But as the economic downturn bites, there will be greater scrutiny of the returns on embryonic research funding—whether in terms of profits to be made on intellectual property rights, or actual delivery of successful therapies to the clinic. A 20- to 30-year delay for dividends in the current economic climate is a long time to wait. In the meantime, Professor Raisman makes an interesting link between regulation in medical science and regulation in banking and the economy: "The creditworthiness of scientific claims," he says, "has no better system of regulation than other derivatives and instruments beloved of financiers, attracting huge bonuses by moving other people's money about."

It is a salutary reminder that the widespread adoption of entrepreneurial and monetarist models from the 1980s onwards for the conduct of medical research is as much due for scrutiny as other failing economic institutions.

Ethical Issues Demand Good, Working Relationships Between Physicians and Patients

Internal Medicine Alert

Internal Medicine Alert is a newsletter published twice monthly by AHC Media LLC.

In this viewpoint, Internal Medicine Alert *interviews J. Randall Curtis, a professor of medicine in the Division of Pulmonary and Critical Care at the University of Washington in Seattle. The American Medical Association maintains that physicians do not have to treat patients unless there is a reasonable chance that such care will be effective, and that patients do not have the right to demand care. Nevertheless saying no to patients who request medical services can be problematic, according to Curtis. The circumstances may be as simple as a patient with an upper-respiratory illness asking for antibiotics even though the physician is reasonably certain that the condition is viral and that antibiotics will not be effective. Or the situation may be as serious and complex as providing life support to terminal patients who have no chance of long-term survival. In all cases, asserts Curtis, doctors who are able to build trust and gain the confidence of their patients through good communication and mediation skills are likely to have more success in guiding patients toward the most effective treatments.*

The American Medical Association's [AMA's] policy in Opinion 2.035 on Futile Care clearly states: "Physicians are not ethically obligated to deliver care that, in their best professional judgment, will not have a reasonable chance of benefiting their patients. Patients should not be given treatments simply because they demand them. . . ."

Likewise, Opinion 2.19 on Unnecessary Medical Services suggests that "Physicians should not provide, prescribe, or seek compensation for medical services that they know are unnecessary."

While the AMA's policy is clear, patient expectations and/or demands for treatment can range from the highly complex to the more common situation, where a patient asks for an antibiotic when the physician thinks his or her ailment is viral. In both cases, physicians can sometimes be challenged by patients.

A Complicated Issue

So, what are the ethics of saying no to patient care?

"I think this is an interesting and a complicated question," [says] J. Randall Curtis, MD, MPH [Master of Public Health], a professor of medicine in the division of pulmonary and critical care at University of Washington. Curtis is the chair of the ethics committee at his hospital, which is Harborview Medical Center.

"And the reason why I say it's complicated is because it depends on the situation and the circumstances. So, I think most physicians believe and practice [with the belief] that physicians are under no obligation to provide therapies that are not indicated just because a patient demands them."

In extreme examples, he says, a patient may demand surgery that the surgeon doesn't think will benefit that patient. Or, a patient requests a bone marrow transplant for a disease "where a bone marrow transplant hasn't been shown to help, then physicians say no to that all the time."

In situations where a requested treatment might cause significant harm or create significant expense—and provide no benefit—it's common for a physician to say no to that treatment.

"I think where it gets more complicated or trickier is when the therapy is not risky and not expensive," Curtis tells *Medical Ethics Advisor* [*MEA*].

"The classic example—there is a patient coming in with what a doctor believes is a viral upper respiratory infection. The doctor doesn't believe antibiotics are indicated, but the patient insists on getting antibiotics, and the doctor feels like 'Well, you know what, this is not expensive therapy and I'm not 100% sure there isn't a bacterial infection. There are some risks involved, but generally, these are pretty safe therapies—and I'm going to go ahead and prescribe them.'"

Curtis says that if you look at the data on the "use of antibiotics for upper respiratory symptoms in otherwise healthy people, the data suggests that doctors will do that, at times," he says. "Whether that's good practice or not, I really think it depends on the scenario. In point of fact, a lot of times, we're not 100% sure that there isn't a bacterial infection."

But if it were one of the physician's family members in that scenario, the physicians probably would not prescribe the antibiotics, he says.

Futile Treatment Can Have Exceptions

The same sort of pattern for physicians follows when the questions surround futile treatments. That is, Curtis says, when the patient requests a very expensive or risky treatment and the physician doesn't feel there will be a benefit, that physician is likely to decline to provide it.

"I think what is more complicated is when the therapy has already been instituted—which happens not infrequently in the intensive care unit—and the situation has worsened. So that, if circumstances have changed where the therapy that's currently being provided—now thought to be futile—and the doctor feels that this therapy should be withdrawn ... that is much more complicated," Curtis tells *MEA*.

In such circumstances, Curtis says that the health care team will enter discussions with the patient, or often, family members, and "try to resolve the conflict without withdrawing life-sustaining treatment against the wishes of a patient or family."

This type of scenario is a common source of ethics consultations at hospitals, in his experience, he says.

In most of those cases, "the recommendations of the ethics committee are, 'Gee, futility is a little hard to determine here. It's hard to be 100% sure if the therapy is futile.' And it may not be therapy that physicians and nurses would want for themselves or their loved ones, but in fact, in this situation it's best just to continue to work on building trust and negotiating with families and continue the therapy," Curtis suggests.

In those rare circumstances, when a hospital decides it will withdraw futile therapy against the wishes of a family, the process for withdrawing life support is often to advise the family that the medical team suggests withdrawing life-sustaining support and give the family 72 hours to find another provider to take on the case, if the family disagrees with the suggestion.

Curtis says he has seen three cases that came to an ethics committee, in which the team decided that the patient was clearly dying, life support was only prolonging death, and that it would be ethically permissible to withdraw life support.

In two of those cases, the decision was made to withdraw care. In one of those circumstances, "this was a family that felt like they had to do everything they could to keep their loved one alive, because of their own religious and cultural beliefs, but in point of fact, they knew this was the right thing. But they had to fight it, and they couldn't be involved in the decision. Once the decision was made [and] it was taken out of their hands, they were actually very appreciative for all the care that their loved one got."

In the third situation, the decision was made to continue care, because otherwise, the family would have been "terribly angry and upset." The decision by the medical team was that "even though it is futile, and even though we know the patient will die, we're not going to withdraw life support against the family's wishes, because it feels like an assault on the family," Curtis recalls.

Building Trust in Difficult Cases

In dealing with patients or their families who may be demanding care, it is important that physicians focus on using good communication skills and good mediation skills, Curtis says.

"In my experience, one of the most important things in this situation is to focus on building trust, so that when there's conflict between patients and clinicians or families and clinicians, it's often a situation where trust has eroded, and I have found it to be very helpful to focus on building trust back, rather than the decision at hand, if that's possible," Curtis tells *MEA*.

While some medical decisions need to be made immediately, other medical decisions can wait for this process to occur, even in the ICU [intensive care unit] setting, he says.

"I think sometimes working on ... understanding the patient's or the family's perspective and why they're making the decisions or demands that they're making and focusing on that aspect of the relationship—putting the decision-making about treatments aside temporarily while doing that can be very helpful," Curtis suggests.

Genetic Testing Forces Parents to Make Difficult Decisions

Karen Kaplan

Karen Kaplan has served as a staff writer for the Los Angeles Times.

Genetic screening tests have been driven by the success of screening for Tay-Sachs disease and are now quite common. According to Kaplan in this viewpoint, while these tests offer knowledge to prospective parents, they do not ensure that parents will make sound decisions with the information that they receive. Parents who learn that their unborn children may be at risk of Gaucher disease may overreact to the news, choose abortion, or decide not to get pregnant at all when in reality the disease is treatable or asymptomatic. Ultimately, Kaplan maintains, decisions must be left to parents, but awareness of the disorders involved can leave them better equipped to make appropriate choices based on screening results.

Thirty-five years after genetic screening was first used to identify babies at risk of being born with debilitating diseases, a new study of a potentially serious but treatable illness among Ashkenazi Jews questions whether such testing has gone too far.

One-quarter of fetuses found to have Gaucher disease were aborted over an eight-year period, even though half of all children with the metabolic disorder will never experience any symptoms, such as pain, organ enlargement and anemia. The rest can lead normal lives with treatment.

Importantly, the researchers found that among couples who met with a Gaucher expert and learned that the disease was treatable, only 8% chose to terminate their pregnancies. All of the couples who didn't have those meetings opted for abortion.

Knowledge but Not Wisdom

The disparity underscores what some experts say is a flaw in genetic testing: It provides a bounty of knowledge that is not necessarily accompanied by wisdom.

The study, published today in the *Journal of the American Medical Association*, tracked nearly 29,000 Israelis who opted to be screened for mutations in their DNA [genetic codes] that could lead to Gaucher disease in their children if they inherit faulty genes from both parents.

Similar screening tests are offered to other specific ethnic groups predisposed to disorders, such as albinism and congenital deafness.

Dr. William R. Wilcox, who treats Gaucher patients at the Medical Genetics Institute at Cedars-Sinai Medical Center in Los Angeles and was not involved in the study, said that given the ambiguity inherent in some genetic tests, they should not be given for diseases that are imminently treatable.

"Personally, that horrifies me," he said. "Why is it there? Because we can do it. But just because we can doesn't mean we should."

Others say abandoning the genetic test would unfairly deny couples genetic information about their offspring.

"It's an opportunity to gain information which some people might want," said Karen Grinzaid, a genetic counselor at Emory University in Atlanta who coordinates care for Gaucher patients. "It's their decision about what they want to do with that information."

Ambiguous Test Results Cloud Parental Thinking

As gene-hunters find more DNA mutations associated with particular diseases, the number of people who will be left grappling with ambiguous results is likely to grow, experts said.

"This is just the tip of the iceberg," Wilcox said. "There will be a time when we have the ability to screen for thousands of diseases in one blood spot. What are you going to terminate for?"

The proliferation of screening tests was largely driven by the success of carrier screening for Tay-Sachs disease, another condition with high incidence among Ashkenazi Jews, or those of Eastern European descent.

Children with Tay-Sachs are unable to process a fatty substance, which builds up in the body and leads to blindness, deafness, paralysis and death by age 4. Since screening for Tay-Sachs carriers began in the early 1970s, the number of cases has dropped by 90%.

Other diseases that Ashkenazi Jews are frequently screened for include Canavan disease and Niemann-Pick disease, which lead to death in early childhood, and debilitating conditions like cystic fibrosis.

Dr. Ephrat Levy-Lahad, director of the Medical Genetics Unit at Shaare Zedek Medical Center in Jerusalem, and colleagues wondered how screening for a relatively mild condition like Gaucher affected couples' family planning decisions.

Gaucher disease is the most common genetic disease among Ashkenazi Jews. Scientists estimate that 6% to 10% of Ashkenazi Jews are carriers of at least one mutation that can lead to the disorder. Roughly 60% of eligible couples in Israel take the screening test, Levy-Lahad said.

But among the eight to 14 Jewish genetic diseases commonly screened for, it is also the most controversial, Grinzaid said. Even knowing which mutations are in a fetus' genes, she said, "we're still not able to predict what's going to be wrong with the child. It can be anywhere from something that presents in childhood, which is treatable, to something that can never present . . . What do you do with that?"

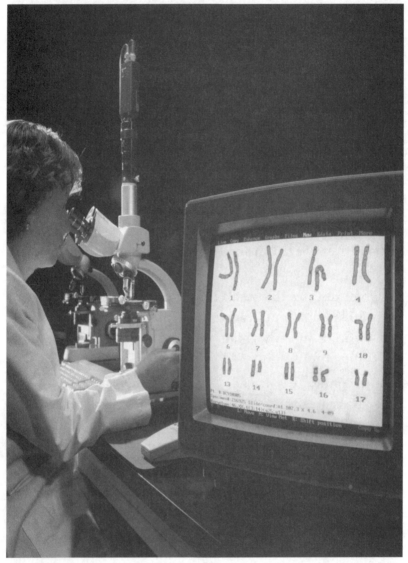

Genetic screening helps identify the risk of certain diseases, which can create a difficult decision for potential parents. © Lester Lefkowitz/Corbis.

Difficult Decisions

Among children who inherit two faulty genes, the most common result is Type 1 Gaucher. Half will become symptomatic at some point in their lives, when harmful amounts of glucocerebroside [an organic compound containing glucose] build up in the spleen, liver, lungs and bone marrow.

Patients can experience pain and suffer from fatigue, although the symptoms can be treated with biweekly infusions of the enzyme that their bodies fail to produce in sufficient quantities. The intravenous infusions take an hour or two at home and cost $100,000 to $400,000 a year.

The researchers surveyed all 10 centers in Israel that screen for Gaucher disease mutations. Between 1995 and 2003, the centers tested about 28,900 people and identified 83 couples where both partners had a mutation.

The researchers were able to interview 65 of the at-risk couples, who had a total of 90 pregnancies. In 68 of those pregnancies, parents opted for an amniocentesis or chorionic villus sampling [types of prenatal tests] to test for Gaucher in their fetuses.

Sixteen of those tests were positive for the disease. In four of the cases, couples opted to terminate their pregnancies.

The researchers surmise that lack of information about Gaucher may have played a role in some of those decisions. Among 13 couples who discussed Gaucher with an expert, one had an abortion. Three couples did not discuss the disease with an expert, and all of them had abortions, according to the study.

One couple, which learned that their particular mutations could lead to one of the most severe—and untreatable—forms of the disease, did not get pregnant. Those types can cause death in early childhood or severe neurological degeneration, and they are no more likely among Ashkenazi Jews than members of other ethnic groups.

In an editorial accompanying the study, Dr. Ernest Beutler said the Gaucher test does little to benefit carriers or their offspring. Instead, he said, it serves mainly to enrich hospitals, testing laboratories and pharmaceutical companies.

"Children are likely to be treated when they don't really need treatment," said Beutler, who chairs the department of molecular and experimental medicine at the Scripps Research Institute in La Jolla [, California]. "You get a child that's 8 or 10 years old and has a slightly enlarged spleen and their hemoglobin is a little low. You can watch a child like that. But once the diagnosis is made, there's pressure to treat. People tend to say, 'Nothing's too good for our child.'"

It Is the Parents' Choice

Just knowing that Gaucher is present can shape the lives of healthy children. "Maybe they won't be allowed to play soccer with their friends," Beutler said. "Maybe they'll wind up being checked by a doctor every two months. It can really change their life and their self-image."

Dr. Robin A. Ely, who raised three children with moderate levels of the disease, said she had counseled couples in the U.S. who were advised by their doctors to abort when genetic tests confirmed a Gaucher diagnosis.

"I tell them, 'This is your choice, but I think it's a mistake,'" said Ely, medical director of the National Gaucher Foundation based in Tucker, Georgia. "It's almost Nazi-like. It's eugenics."

But what may seem like a mistake to one family may be the right choice for another.

For instance, the high cost of enzyme replacement therapy may tilt some couples toward abortion, Levy-Lahad said. Insurance plans in the United States typically cover the treatment, but patients whose policies include a lifetime cap may run into trouble.

Cost was probably not a factor for couples in the study because the treatment is covered by Israel's national health insurance.

One of the couples interviewed by researchers said they were concerned about how they would pay for treatment if they left the country. However, they elected to carry their Gaucher baby to term.

For Further Discussion

1. Does Mary Shelley seem to be grounded in scientific theory, or is her grasp of contemporary eighteenth- and nineteenth-century science incomplete? (See Nitchie, Florescu.)

2. Based on the articles in Chapter 2, is *Frankenstein* a warning against all scientific experimentation or only against unchecked and misguided research?

3. Mary Shelley's mother, Mary Wollstonecraft, was a famous early feminist. How is *Frankenstein* a reflection of feminist thought about the sciences? (See Franklin, Mellor.)

4. Is *Frankenstein* an appropriate warning to today's scientists, or is it misguided to take the novel seriously as an ethics text for today's experimenters in biotechnology? (See Davies, Bishop, Turney, Clayton.)

5. Based on the articles in Chapter 3, do you think contemporary biotechnology is on the right track or is it spiraling out of control?

6. A key scene in *Frankenstein* occurs when Victor refuses to honor his creature's request and destroys the mate he is constructing for the monster. Does the *Internal Medicine Alert* article properly justify a doctor's decision to say no to a patient?

For Further Reading

Emily Brontë, *Wuthering Heights*. 1847.

Philip K. Dick, *Do Androids Dream of Electric Sheep?* 1968.

William Godwin, *Things as They Are; or, The Adventures of Caleb Williams*. 1794.

Aldous Huxley, *Brave New World*. 1932.

Ann Radcliffe, *The Italian; or, The Confessional of the Black Penitents: A Romance*. 1797.

Mary Shelley, *Falkner: A Novel*. 1837.

————, *The Last Man*. 1826.

————, *Lodore*. 1835.

————, *Mathilda*. Ed. Elizabeth Nitchie. Chapel Hill: University of North Carolina Press, 1959.

————, *Valperga*. 1823.

Robert Louis Stevenson, *The Strange Case of Dr Jekyll and Mr Hyde*. 1886.

Bram Stoker, *Dracula*. 1897.

H.G. Wells, *The Island of Dr. Moreau*. 1896.

Bibliography

Books

Stephen Bann	*Frankenstein, Creation, and Monstrosity.* London: Reaktion Books, 1994.
Jonathan Baron	*Against Bioethics.* Cambridge, MA: MIT Press, 2006.
Harold Bloom	*Frankenstein.* Philadelphia: Chelsea House, 2004.
Howard Brody	*The Future of Bioethics.* Oxford: Oxford University Press, 2009.
H. Tristram Engelhardt	*Global Bioethics: The Collapse of Consensus.* Salem, MA: M & M Scrivener Press, 2006.
Leslie Fiedler	*Tyranny of the Normal: Essays on Bioethics, Theology & Myth.* Boston: D.R. Godine, 1996.
David E. Guinn	*Handbook of Bioethics and Religion.* Oxford: Oxford University Press, 2006.
John Harris	*Bioethics.* New York: Oxford University Press, 2001.
Cecil Helman	*The Body of Frankenstein's Monster: Essays in Myth and Medicine.* New York: W.W. Norton, 1992.

Susan Tyler Hitchcock

Frankenstein: A Cultural History. New York: W.W. Norton, 2007.

Dorothy Hoobler and Thomas Hoobler

The Monsters: Mary Shelley and the Curse of Frankenstein. New York: Little, Brown, 2006.

Christa Knellwolf and Jane R. Goodall

Frankenstein's Science: Experimentation and Discovery in Romantic Culture, 1780–1830. Aldershot, UK: Ashgate, 2008.

Susan E. Lederer, Elizabeth Fee, and Patricia Tuohy

Frankenstein: Penetrating the Secrets of Nature; An Exhibition by the National Library of Medicine. New Brunswick, NJ: Rutgers University Press, 2002.

George Lewis Levine and U.C. Knoepflmacher

The Endurance of "Frankenstein": Essays on Mary Shelley's Novel. Berkeley: University of California Press, 1979.

Ronald A. Lindsay

Future Bioethics: Overcoming Taboos, Myths, and Dogmas. Amherst, NY: Prometheus Books, 2008.

Nicholas Marsh

Mary Shelley: Frankenstein. Basingstoke, UK: Palgrave Macmillan, 2009.

Tim Marshall

Murdering to Dissect: Grave-Robbing, "Frankenstein" and the Anatomy Literature. Manchester: Manchester University Press, 1995.

Colin McGinn

Ethics, Evil, and Fiction. Oxford: Clarendon Press, 1997.

Jonathan D. Moreno	*Is There an Ethicist in the House?: On the Cutting Edge of Bioethics.* Bloomington: Indiana University Press, 2005.
Barry R. Schaller	*Understanding Bioethics and the Law: The Promises and Perils of the Brave New World of Biotechnology.* Westport, CT: Praeger, 2008.
Mary Shelley	*Frankenstein: The 1818 Text, Contexts, Nineteenth-Century Responses, Modern Criticism.* Ed. J. Paul Hunter. New York: W.W. Norton, 1996.
David J. Skal	*Screams of Reason: Mad Science and Modern Culture.* New York: W.W. Norton, 1998.
Johanna M. Smith	*Mary Shelley.* New York: Twayne Publishers, 1996.
Martin Tropp	*Mary Shelley's Monster.* Boston: Houghton Mifflin, 1976.
Judith Wilt	*Making Humans: Complete Texts with Introduction, Historical Contexts, Critical Essays.* Boston: Houghton Mifflin, 2003.

Periodicals

Glen Scott Allen	"Master Mechanics & Evil Wizards: Science and the American Imagination from Frankenstein to Sputnik," *Massachusetts Review*, vol. 33, no. 4, Winter 1992.

Peter Brooks

"Godlike Science/Unhallowed Arts: Language and Monstrosity in *Frankenstein*," *New Literary History*, vol. 9, no. 3, Spring 1978.

Kevin Bushweller

"Frankenstein, Dolly, and Ethics," *American School Board Journal*, vol. 185, no. 7, July 1998.

Courtney S. Campbell

"Biotechnology and the Fear of Frankenstein," *Cambridge Quarterly of Healthcare Ethics*, vol. 12, no. 4, 2003.

S. Finger and M.B. Law

"Karl August Weinhold and His 'Science' in the Era of Mary Shelley's Frankenstein: Experiments on Electricity and the Restoration of Life," *Journal of the History of Medicine and Allied Sciences*, vol. 53, no. 2, April 1998.

Roslynn Haynes

"From Alchemy to Artificial Intelligence: Stereotypes of the Scientist in Western Literature," *Public Understanding of Science*, vol. 12, no. 3, 2003.

R.G. Hudson

"A Purposeless History and a 'Brave New World' for Animals," *Social Epistemology*, vol. 12, no. 2, 1998.

James A. Metcalf

"Victor Frankenstein May Be a 'Dead-Beat' Dad, But He Offers Lessons for Health Science Students," *Radical Pedagogy*, vol. 9, no. 1, 2007.

Pedro J. Morgado   "Colorectal Surgery in the Twenty-first Century and Frankenstein's Shadow," *Diseases of the Colon and Rectum*, vol. 46, no. 4, April 2003.

Michael Mulka   "Frankenstein and the Debate over Embryo Research," *Science, Technology, and Human Values*, vol. 21, no. 2, 1996.

B.E. Rollin   "'The Frankenstein Thing': The Moral Impact of Genetic Engineering of Agricultural Animals on Society and Future Science," *Basic Life Sciences*, vol. 37, 1986.

Megan Stern   "Dystopian Anxieties Versus Utopian Ideals: Medicine from *Frankenstein* to the Visible Human Project and Body Worlds," *Science as Culture*, vol. 15, no. 1, March 2006.

Paul Winkelman   "Frankenstein Goes to Engineering School," *European Journal of Engineering Education*, vol. 31, no. 4, August 2006.

Index

DATE DUE

FOLLETT